Cha Dao

of related interest

Seeking the Spirit of The Book of Change
8 Days to Mastering a Shamanic Yijing (I Ching) Prediction System
Master Zhongxian Wu
ISBN 978 1 84819 020 7

Bagua Daoyin
A Unique Branch of Daoist Learning, A Secret Skill of the Palace
He Jinghan
Translated by David Alexander
ISBN 978 1 84819 009 2

The Way of Tea,

Tea as a Way of Life

Cha Dao

By Solala Towler

SINGING DRAGON
LONDON AND PHILADELPHIA

First published in 2010
by Singing Dragon
an imprint of Jessica Kingsley Publishers
116 Pentonville Road
London N1 9JB, UK
and
400 Market Street, Suite 400
Philadelphia, PA 19106, USA

www.singing-dragon.com

Copyright © Solala Towler 2010

Library of Congress Cataloging in Publication Data
A CIP catalog record for this book is available from the Library of Congress

British Library Cataloguing in Publication Data
A CIP catalogue record for this book is available from the British Library

ISBN 978 1 84819 032 0

Contents

Introduction

Although titled *The Way of Tea*, this book is about much more than tea alone, for it is impossible to separate Daoist philosophy from the practice or Way of Tea. Daoist philosophy permeates every aspect of the Way of Tea. And so this book, besides being a book about the Way of Tea, has also an element of a Daoist primer. You will find chapters on Wu Wei or non-striving, the Uncarved Block or innate naturalness, and on the Value of Worthlessness. This is because all of these aspects of Daoist thought and practice both contribute to, and are informed by, the Way of Tea. There is also a chapter on the Japanese version of the Way of Tea, in which the Daoist practice of Tea Mind and of effortless attainment evolved into the sublime practice of Zen.

The idea for writing this book came about one morning as my partner Shanti ran breathlessly around getting ready for work, making her lunch, and then eating her breakfast while standing at the counter. She looked over at me, with teacup in hand, slowly immersing myself in the day, and said, "Wow, look at you, sitting down with a hot cup of tea while I rush around and eat my breakfast standing up in the kitchen. You really live your life by the Way of Tea, don't you?"

So I thought, yes, I do try to live my whole life according to Tea Mind. Why don't I write a book about that? So here it is, my small contribution to the philosophy and practice of the Way of Tea.

I have been publishing *The Empty Vessel*, a journal of Daoist thought and practice, since 1993. I have had the opportunity to meet and interact with many masters, teachers and students of the Dao. Since 1998 I have led tours to China where we visit Daoist temples up in the sacred mountains of China and do our qigong practice there, in the birthplace of qigong and Daoism.

And, of course, I have drunk a lot of tea. I have drunk tea in teahouses at Daoist and Buddhist temples, Chinese and Tibetan restaurants, airports, and countless Chinese hotel rooms; I have drunk tea in beautiful green Oregon at the Tao of Tea teahouse in Portland, with my friend and tea master Zhongxian Wu, and at my beloved home in Eugene.

To Daoists, drinking tea is not merely imbibing a hot cup of water with some leaves floating in it. As you will see in the coming chapters, it is also about how to live each moment of our life, how we approach the very substance of our soul, as well as the ongoing evolution of our spirit. It is part of how we find our place within the ever-changing, ever-shifting universe, which the ancient Chinese called Dao.

Solala Towler
Abode of the Eternal Dao
Eugene, OR
Year of the Yang Gold Tiger

1

Cha Dao

The Way of Tea

This book is about the art and practice of drinking tea. What could be simpler, you may ask, than making and drinking a cup of tea? But for Chinese and Japanese people, serving and drinking tea is about much more than slapping a teabag into a cup of boiling water and drinking it down. The art and practice of drinking tea is rooted in Daoism and emerged from a philosophy that honored living a life of grace and elegance, of balance and harmony, of fulfillment and enjoyment.

The Chinese character for tea is *cha*.茶 It is composed of three parts. The top one represents plants. The middle one represents human or person. The bottom one means wood or "being rooted." Thus the true meaning of cha or tea could mean something like "the plant that gives humans a sense of being rooted or balanced."

Daoism (Taoism) is the native philosophy of China, going back thousands of years and having its roots in ancient shamanism (*wu*). Most people have heard about the Dao through the book by Laozi (Lao Tzu) called the *Daodejing* (*Tao de Ching*), written over 2500 years ago. In it Laozi, or Old Boy as he is called in China, writes, in eighty-one short and concise chapters, a primer on how to live a balanced and harmonious life, in accordance with the basic laws of nature. As a matter of fact, nature may be used in place of the term Dao. By nature he means the vast, ever-changing, organic nature of the universe and our place in it.

Laozi describes the Dao as:

Something mysteriously formed,
Born before heaven and earth.
In the silence and the void,
Standing alone and unchanging,
Ever present and in motion.
It is the Mother of both heaven and earth.
I do not know its name
And so I call it "Dao."

(Chapter 25)

The *Daodejing* has been used, down through the centuries, as a treatise for governing a country as well as a manual for spiritual self-cultivation (*xiulian*). It was originally written in archaic Chinese and can be translated in many different ways, depending on the translator's knowledge of not only Chinese, but also the language of the Daoist cultivation techniques that it describes. There are many different versions in English as well as other languages. I would suggest you take a look at several and do a comparison. In this way you will be able to get a true flavor of what the Old Boy is talking about. All the quotes from the *Daodejing*, except for one, are mine.

A contemporary book describing Daoism in China tells us that Daoism

is consistent with that of ancient Chinese philosophy; its principles—including the

> worship of nature, striving for inner purity,
> and reduction of personal desire—have been
> important aesthetic goals for Chinese people
> for tens of centuries.[1]

Daoism, then, has its roots in ancient Chinese thought about nature and our place in it. It has had its hand in almost every aspect of Chinese culture—from painting, poetry, landscape design, music and martial arts (where the principles of "overcoming the hard with the soft" and "controlling the moving with the still" come into play),[2] to food preparation, herbal medicine, acupuncture, qigong and internal alchemy. And, of course, tea.

Yet Daoism is much more than that. It is a way of living in the world—being intensely *engaged* with life yet not being attached to the outcome of any endeavor. In Daoism we learn that everything that is alive (this includes animals, plants, water and even mountains) is filled with *qi* (chee) or basic live essence. Not only that but also our own personal qi is able to interact with the qi of trees, plants, rivers, oceans and mountains.

One of my teachers, Master Hua-Ching Ni, says:

> If you trace the meaning of the word "Daoist"
> it only means someone who follows Dao. Do
> you know what that means? It means flowing
> in oneness with life, naturally, without the
> impositions of fabricated notions that create
> separation through differentiation and division.
> People who follow Dao have chosen to develop
> naturally rather than be programmed by anyone
> or any group.[3]

In China Daoism is divided into two categories or groups— *daojio* or religious Daoism and *daojia* or philosophical Daoism. The religious form of Daoism includes the Quanzhen School or Eternal Reality sect, which is organized in a monastic system of vegetarian, celibate monks and nuns. Then there is the Tienshi or Heavenly Master sect, in which monks and nuns often have families and live outside the temple. The religious form of Daoism has been heavily influenced by Buddhism and is a priestly or liturgical form of Daoism with lots of ceremonies and chanting of scripture (including the *Daodejing*, which is chanted daily) and many other priestly functions such as funerals or ceremonies for the benefit and well-being of the community. It was formed in the second century CE.

The other form of Daoism is what some people call philosophical Daoism or Huang-Lao Daoism. This term is one that has been used since the Han dynasty (206 BCE to 220 CE) to describe the school of thought originating with Laozi and Zhuangzi (Chuang Tzu). This is the most ancient Daoist system and the one favored by most people in the West.

There is a lot of argument in Western scholarly circles about whether these two terms are correct and whether one can separate the two approaches to Daoism in this way. But in my travels in China and with my Chinese Daoist friends there seems to be an agreement that there really are two distinct strains of Daoism though there is also considerable overlap. For instance the religious Daoists study the works of Laozi and Zhuangzi as well as other ancient Daoist philosophers like Lieh Tzu. As mentioned earlier, the chanting of the *Daodejing* is part of their regular ceremonies. They also do their own practices such as meditation, tai chi, qigong and other forms of internal alchemy practices, as do the followers of the Huang-Lao school. But, on the other hand, the *daojia* people are not as involved with the religious form of practice and primarily do the self-cultivation practices.

The term Daoist itself can be problematical also. The actual term was something that was created by Western scholars in the 1840s. The Chinese did not use this term and you will not find it anywhere in the writings of Laozi or Zhuangzi. Indeed there are so many different strands and approaches to Daoism in China that there is actually no clear definition of Daoism there.

Is someone a Daoist who is an ordained priest in the Daoist religion or who attends regular services in a Daoist temple? Or is it someone who reads Daoist works and does practices that are often associated with Daoism such as qigong, tai chi (tai ji) or internal alchemy meditation? Or is it a person who tries, in their own way, to follow the Dao?

Master Ni has this to say:

> The word "Tao" is translated in various ways in Western languages, and people who follow the Tao are called "Taoists." Both words are wrongly interpreted because Tao is not another "ism," nor can anyone be called a "Taoist," because Tao is just the plain, unadorned natural truth.[4]

Whatever terminology you want to give it, to me a Daoist is someone who is following the teachings of the ancient achieved masters, using the principles of *wu wei* and non-striving, of being natural and unhurried, of being in tune with their own energetic and emotional system, who is humble and open to change in every moment, and one who is able to use every experience in their life for their own self-cultivation. This is, of course, a personal interpretation but one that I have come to after almost twenty years of study and practice. As the Dao itself is not just for Chinese people, one does not have to be Chinese to understand and utilize its teachings and practices.

As tea master Kakuzo Okakura says: "The art of life lies in a constant readjustment to our surroundings. Taoism accepts the mundane as it is and, unlike the Confucians and the Buddhists, tries to find beauty in our world of woe and worry."[5] This approach to life encompasses much more than tea but the Way of

Tea can be used as a useful metaphor in describing a way to live one's life in a harmonious, relaxed and mindful way.

John Blofeld says: "The world today is so full of distractions that mindfulness, which must have come about spontaneously in time gone by, has to be cultivated."[6] This is true and one of the most important reasons to begin a practice like tai chi (tai ji) or qigong (chee gung).

So, you may ask, what does all of this have to do with the Way of Tea? Ah, but it has *everything* to do with the Art and Way of Tea! The Way or Dao of Tea is a philosophy and practice of living a life that is full yet not overwhelming, lived at a slow pace yet in an extremely productive fashion, full of magic and miracles yet still solidly grounded; it is a way of living, open to every subtle shift in the world around and within us and at the same time is strong enough to give us the ability to fill our sails with the winds of adversity and fly over the oftentimes rough waters of life.

There are important principles to this way of life, this Way of Tea. There are several in this chapter. You can read about some more in Chapters 6, 8 and 10 on Wu Wei, the Uncarved Block and the Value of Worthlessness.

1 Go slowly

Almost all Daoist practices, from tai chi or qigong movement to sexual practices, involve slowing down and being with the present eternal moment. The soft, slow movements of tai chi and qigong may seem like dancing in slow motion but within the practitioner great tides and turns of energy or *qi* are flowing within and around them.

In the introduction to Lu Yu's *Classic of Tea*, translated by Francis Ross Carpenter, we read:

> perhaps most importantly, tea epitomizes the Chinese attitude toward time and change. To

the Westerner, life has always seemed very linear. Today must somehow improve upon yesterday and tomorrow must extend and build upon today. The Chinese have taken a more cyclic view of their world. The Westerner has danced to an insistent beat called "progress," the Chinese, to a rhythm of natural movement.

Natural movement had several implications for the early Chinese, none of which denied the fact of change. One such implication was that standstill and rest are a part of change. The growth and development of what is unnatural (and therefore wrong) is not change but its very antithesis. Central to the Chinese concept is the idea of return. To get back to the starting point and the source of one's strength was of the essence of change.[7]

Going slowly is the key to being a healthy person. By rushing around, guzzling high caffeine coffee all day, many people come home at the end of the day and just collapse in front of the television, a soul-deadening practice, and one that leads to becoming disconnected to real life.

Here is something from Master Wu about this.

One of the major differences I have noticed between Chinese and American lifestyles is the way time is handled. When I first came [to America], it was a big shock to see that everyone had a schedule book. As I started working with people in the U.S., I found that everything had to be planned ahead. I felt that I could not enjoy the moment when I tried doing this. I had to think about what I would be doing in the next hour, even in the next minute. It seemed to me that one day's life was not whole. It was divided into many small pieces. I have tried to not make too many plans in a day, and I have never used a schedule book in all my time here. I am trying to maintain my daily life in oneness.

When I worked eight hours a day as an engineer in China, I didn't feel rushed or stressed because I stayed in one place—no car, no going out for anything, no leaving for appointments. Everything was there. During break times I could drink my tea (I had a tea set in my office) and read a book. I had time to practice my Qigong and martial arts, play my music, and write my Qigong books after work. I could enjoy myself without rushing. When the physical body is more settled down, the heart/mind will be more settled down.[8]

In the Way of Tea we begin each day in as slow and harmonious a fashion as possible. Tea Mind means brewing and drinking tea in a slow and unhurried manner. If you are someone who has to be up and out the door in as short a time as possible, this can be very challenging. But really, it takes only a few minutes to make tea. Even if you give yourself only 15–20 minutes to make and drink your tea, you can still achieve a period of calmness and serenity as you do so. Is that not a great way to start your day?

It is when we slow down that we can be better able to notice the small and often fleeting moments that add up to a life. Life is not one big party after another, nor is it one terrible tragedy after another either. Much of the time our lives may seem boring or even trivial. But that is only when we are programmed, by television or unreal expectations, that life will always be exciting and fulfilling or else we are missing something grand and important.

We must learn to treasure the small moments as well as the grand ones. We must be content to make small steps toward our goals. We must not be attached to outcomes.

Laozi says:

> The sage practices non-action.
> She teaches by not speaking,
> Achieves in all things while undertaking nothing,
> Creates but does not take credit,
> Acts but does not defend,
> Accomplishes much while not claiming merit.
> Because she claims no merit,
> Her work will last forever.

(Chapter 2)

On a trip to China in 2006 my group and I worked with Wang Chingwei, a Daoist monk on Hua Shan (Flower Mountain), one of China's sacred Daoist mountains. He lived at a small temple at the top of this rugged mountain, but came down to the town of Hua Shan to teach us some qigong and then to lead us back up the mountain to his home. Like most Daoist monks and nuns, he was dressed in traditional clothing, a style that dates back hundreds of years, with his long hair gathered into a topknot on the top of his head and held there with a jade stickpin. He smelled, as most mountain Daoists do, like smoke and caves and something I could not quite put my finger on. It was a wild smell though, one that clearly does not come from living in cities and warm houses with indoor plumbing.

He was very gracious and, even though his accent was almost impenetrable to our guide from Xian, he was able to teach us a simple qigong form and also demonstrate for us an elegant and very powerful form that he himself practiced. Everybody liked him and trusted him to take us up the mountain on the very steep and often quite dangerous trails there.

But the thing about him that most impressed me was how slow and easy he was the whole time we were with him. He did not strut, as some Daoist monks do. He did not even walk from place to place; he *ambled*, like he had all the time in the world. Which, in fact, being a Daoist and a bit of a recluse, he did. He moved so slowly and effortlessly that I was in awe of him. I tried to follow his example on the following days as we hiked around the town and along the mountain trails but my own Western fascination with speed often overcame me and I found myself tramping along as if I were in a race.

Another experience on that trip taught me more about the value of going slowly. It was when we were visiting the Daoist mountains outside of Chengdu, on our way up to a temple we were staying at near the top. It was a very warm day and, unlike the rugged and dry mountains of Hua Shan, we were in a thick forest, almost a jungle. It was very hot and humid and, for some reason, instead of taking the cable car *up* the mountain and then hiking *down* to our temple our guide had us hike *up* the mountain and, some days later, take the cable car *down*.

Part way up the mountain we ran into a group of porters, who were very funny people, all outfitted with a uniform that proclaimed them as official porters and to be trusted with our things. We haggled with them a bit and agreed on some small price to take all our backpacks up the mountain for us, leaving us to sweat our way up the mountain unencumbered with heavy, hot loads. They even offered to carry *us* up the mountain but at that we demurred. They loaded our backpacks onto several large slings and, one man on each end, began walking lightly up the mountain, laughing loudly, as I imagined, at what a great deal they were getting for carrying a few tiny backpacks!

They were such a jolly bunch, all wearing tattered green sneakers. No hiking boots for those guys! Trails in China, even in the highest mountains, are not like trails in the West. For some reason the Chinese like to walk up steps. And so hundreds and even thousands of steps are carved, sometimes into solid rock, all the way up and all the way down. This, to me, actually makes it harder to hike up the mountains, as the steps are of unequal heights and often broken and crumbly.

So there I was, trudging up the steps at a somewhat quick speed, forgetting entirely about my decision to slow down, when one of the porters said to me, "Manzou, manzou. Go slowly, go slowly." It was then that I saw the secret of the porters—how they made it up and down the mountain all day in their tattered sneakers. They took their time. They went slowly. They laughed a lot and even stopped for cigarette breaks fairly often. In the mountains there are no roads. Everything, and I mean everything—from food and water to building materials, even toilet paper—is carried on the backs of porters. And when they get to the top, sometimes they just sit themselves down, lay their heads down on their packs and take a nap! (I never cease to be amazed at how gifted the Chinese are at taking naps in the most noisy and crowded places. I envy their ability to just let go and drift off to sleep in the middle of a crowd or on the desk in their office or even behind the counter at a store.)

Like climbing a mountain, the beauty of drinking tea is that, unlike a cold beer or glass of water, you cannot just guzzle it down. It is hot and so you have to sip it, slowly. This is a good thing.

As Master Wu tells us:

> In Chinese, we use the character *Man* to stand for this way of life. *Man* is composed of the left radical for heart and right radical for graceful and prolonged. It is an image of a person taking a long time to enjoy a graceful life with the heart.
>
> Life here in America is so different from the life I had in China. My first feeling about life in American culture is that life is a rush. In China, the traditional way of life is called *Man*, which

means that everything should slow down. *Man* is a way of meditating, and it is also the way of a natural lifestyle. In Chinese, *Man* carries more meanings than its literal translation into English as "slow." It includes the experience of relaxing, enjoying oneself and—through an intentional, or mindful, leisureliness—remaining calm in all actions and in all situations. This is the essential experience gained over thousands of years by ancient Chinese people living a natural lifestyle. Now, modern China is being widely affected by western culture and daily life is getting more and more rushed.

Traditionally, in China, when we start to eat, we say *"Manchi"*—Eat slowly—in the same way the French say *"Bon appetit."* And instead of saying goodbye in China, we say *"Manzou"*—Go slowly. Although I am living in a continually modernizing world, I want to maintain the attitude of enjoying my life; therefore, I often remind myself of my ancient ancestors' wisdom: *Man*, slow down, no rush, enjoy the moment.[9]

2 Naturalness

Another term for naturalness in Daoism is the Uncarved Block (or *P'u* in Chinese) and it is an essential element of Daoist philosophy and practice. It is the concept of the simple, uncluttered and natural man and woman and their way of life. This way of being in the world is in perfect accord, of course, with the teachings of Laozi and Zhuangzi.

In the *Daodejing* we read:

> Fame or one's life: Which is more important?
> Self or wealth: Which is more precious?
> Gain or loss: Which is more harmful?

> Those who love excess will suffer greatly.
> Those who hoard will suffer heavy losses.
> Those who know when they have enough
>   will not find themselves in trouble.
> They will endure forever.

(Chapter 44)

The ancient Daoists not only were content to live simple, natural lives but also actually felt there was a solid advantage to doing so. It is not necessary to drop out and live in the mountains away from the world in order to live a simple, natural life. What we are actually talking about is an *internal* state of simplicity and naturalness. We may be involved in all kinds of things, from running a large clinic to teaching a group of children or overseeing a complicated business. Yet all of this need not stop us from having internal simplicity and naturalness.

It is when we allow outside pressures and complications to take up residence within us that we run into trouble and lose our sense of safety and spontaneity, which to Daoists is very serious indeed.

Hua-Ching Ni says: "An undistorted human life is the real model of all universal truth."[10] Nowadays the term "natural" is tossed about, with very few people even knowing what it means. How is it possible to be natural in this non-natural world of ours? How is possible to live our lives out in a real and authentic fashion? How is it possible to know how to be natural and in the moment when the whole world is going at a hundred miles a minute all around us?

Laozi says:

> Practice not-doing (wu wei).
> Accomplish your work without trying.
> Taste that which has no taste.
> Reduce the large to small.
> Make more into less.
> Respond to injury with kindness.
> Deal with difficulties before they become difficult.
> Find greatness in small things.
>
> (Chapter 63)

In the path of Dao we work on discovering and claiming what is called our Authentic Self (*zi ran*). What is this authentic self? There are many paths to understanding who we really are.

Daoists, like Zen practitioners, believe in learning by direct experience. When Laozi says "Know the yang but hold to the yin," one of the things he is talking about is the difference between the yang world of doing and the yin world of being. The yang world is what holds our attention so much of the time. It is the external world of achievement and accomplishment and fame and fortune. The yin world, on the other hand, is the internal, quiet world of simply being in the eternal moment of our authentic natural self. Of course this can be a challenge in our yang-dominated world. But this is what the Way of Tea is all about.

In the Way of Tea we are taking time out of the business of the yang world and slowing down to take some time in the yin world. Coffee—with its high caffeine content and lifestyle of pushing oneself to produce more, and more quickly—is the yang while the slow and steady lifestyle of the tea drinker lets things take their course. The sage, says Laozi, is the one who does nothing yet nothing is left undone.

Of course this is a generalization. Not all coffee drinkers are speedy, achievement-oriented people and not all tea drinkers are mellow, let it flow types. But the analogy that is true is that, by taking time out of the rush of the day to savor some "timeless time" in the Way of Tea, we can perhaps allow ourselves to feel that part of ourselves that is timeless and limitless and eternal.

There are other ways to achieve this as well—meditation for one. By this I mean not only formal meditation but also that attitude of being aware and awake and authentic in our being in as many ways as is possible for us to be.

Hua-Ching Ni says: "By restoring and invigorating the natural awareness in the heart of our being we transform life into a sacred expression of our unity with all aspects of the universe."[11] In Daoism meditation and the meditative life is called "Embracing the One," meaning getting in touch with and embracing the one indivisible reality that is the foundation of everything.

Laozi says, about the person who lives their life in this fashion:

This is why the sage embraces the one,
And serves as a model for everything under heaven.
In not showing off
She is seen by everyone.
In not being self-satisfied,
She is prominent.
In not being too aggressive
She accomplishes all her tasks.
In not boasting
She is admired by all.
Because she does not contend
No one contends with her.
The ancients said:
To yield is to become whole.

(Chapter 22)

3 Flexibility and the watercourse way

Daoists are big believers in the quality of flexibility. In the *Daodejing* we find the following chapter:

> When we are born we are soft and weak.
> When we die we are rigid and stiff.
> When grass and trees are young
> They are soft and pliable.
> When they die they are dry and brittle.
> Therefore, stiffness and inflexibility
> Belong to death
> While soft and yielding
> Belong to life.
>
> (Chapter 76)

This quality of flexibility is very strong throughout the philosophy and practice of Daoism. Concepts such as the soft prevailing over the hard, yielding and overcoming, knowing the yang but holding to the yin, and the watercourse way are found all through Daoist teachings. Flexibility is also the basis for being able to deal with life's challenges in a healthy and non-stressful way.

The *Daodejing* uses water as a symbol of the free flowingness and humbleness of the sage or self-realized person.

> Under heaven there is nothing
>   softer and more yielding than water.
> Yet for attacking the stiff and unyielding,
>   there is nothing better;
> There is nothing that can replace it.
>
> (Chapter 78)

And:

> The highest good is like water.
> Water benefits the ten thousand beings
> Yet it does not strive.
> It flows into places people reject
> And so is like the Dao.

(Chapter 8)

Daoist teachings about water—being soft and yielding yet able to cut through solid rock; willing to flow into the lowest, most humble areas; having the ability to adapt to whatever shape it finds itself in—these are also qualities of the sage or self-realized person. It is in our ability to be flexible and "go with the flow" of the watercourse way that we find ourselves being supported by the Dao.

It is when we tighten up, when we forget to breathe—deeply and from the belly, when we close our minds to new experiences and knowledge, when we are so sure that we are right and others are wrong that we have no room within us for change, when we become hard and unyielding, that we align ourselves with death. It is in yielding to that soft, pliable, humble and flexible part of our being that we will be better able to enjoy our lives, with all their challenges and exciting changes.

"Those who speak do not know," says Laozi, "and those who know do not speak." In exalting ourselves and our pitiful amount of knowledge we miss the opportunity to learn and better our understanding of the world and our place in it (see Chapter 9, The Man Who Knew Too Much).

Zhuangzi talks about a drunken man who, when the cart he is riding tips over and throws him out, does not injure himself because his body is so loose (see Chapter 6). Now it is not necessary that we become alcoholics to benefit in the same way. Instead, it is important to keep a loose and open and flexible spirit so that we can enjoy our life and the myriad challenges that occur.

By remaining flexible we can dance with the changes of life rather than tighten up and resist them. It is when we become tight and resistant that we suffer. When we find ourselves in situations or thought processes that cause us to tighten inside that we must remember to breathe and soften. Remember, softness and yielding are connected to life while stiffness and inflexibility are connected to death.

Tea Mind, then, is something that goes beyond merely enjoying a cup of hot tea. It is a way of being in the world, a way of living a life of grace and gratitude, of being able to see the sacred in the seemingly mundane and of being open to magic, mystery and miracles. Tea Mind is a state of being in accordance with the ancient teachings of the Dao, thereby bringing them into our life in a concrete and useful way. Tea Mind is a way to bring ourselves in harmony with the greater world of being, both within as well as without us.

Tea drinking involves all five of the *wu xing* or Five Transformational Phases—wood, fire, earth, metal or gold (in other systems this correlates with air) and water. We heat water with fire then pour it into a clay (from the earth) pot containing tea leaves (wood). We then breathe in the aroma of the resulting tea. In this way, this simple act of preparing tea connects us to all five elements of creation.

In the following chapters we will explore more how this Tea Mind was used in Japan, a culture that was profoundly influenced by China, a short history of tea in Asia as well as a few more principles of Daoist philosophy. We will also hear some tea stories, some based on historical events, others written in the spirit of Tea Mind.

Notes

1. Wang Yi'e (2006) *Daoism in China*, p.11.
2. Ibid, p.122.
3. Hua-Ching Ni (1987) *The Gentle Path of Spiritual Progress*, p.5.
4. Ibid, p.302.

5. Kakuzo Okakura (2001) *The Book of Tea*, p.42.

6. John Blofeld (1985) *The Chinese Art of Tea*, p.xii.

7. Lu Yu, *The Classic of Tea*, p.8.

8. Zhongxian Wu (2008), *Vital Breath of the Dao*, p.4.

9. Ibid, p.3.

10. Hua-Ching Ni (1979) *Tao: The Subtle Universal Law and the Integral Way of Life*, p.110.

11. Ibid, p.95.

2

A Brief History
of Tea in China

The origins of tea

The story of tea in China, like many other aspects of Chinese ancient history, lies shrouded in myth and legend. According to Beatrice Hohenegger in her book *Liquid Jade*:

> The ancient Chinese healers believed that the spirit and essence of the Great Mother Goddess flowed from the center of the Earth into plants and minerals. They collected and experimented with herbs and stones thought to contain varying degrees of "soul substance," which was beneficial for health and longevity. The plants and stones that stored up the greatest amount of soul substance were the ones with "good

color." Jade, for example, was considered very powerful on account of its brilliant shades of green. The good color may be what attracted the healers also to the luscious, evergreen tea plant and might explain why, in China, tea as a beverage came to be known as the "froth of the liquid jade," in honor of the much revered magical stone.[1]

In any case, the origins of how humans began drinking this liquid jade can be presented by two main stories, one about the legendary sage and ruler Shen Nong and the other about the Indian Buddhist teacher Bodhidharma.

Shen Nong, whose name can be translated as the Divine Farmer, lived around 5000 years ago. He is said to have taught his people how to farm and is credited with creating the first wooden plow. From this the primarily agrarian culture of the Chinese came forth.

But, more importantly for our story, he is credited with discovering tea. Interestingly enough, this discovery was only a by-product of his intense study of herbs. Shen Nong is the father of Chinese herbalism and his work, the *Shen Nong Ben Cao Jing* or *Shen Nong's Herbal Classic*, is still used today. The book lists 365 formulas and herbal preparations derived from plant, animal and mineral sources.

The really interesting thing about Shen Nong and his study of herbs and medicines is that he is said to have tasted each herb or medicine personally. Apparently he was poisoned many times but he also ate so many beneficial herbs and medicines that he was able to recover each time. Some stories even describe him as having a transparent stomach, so that he could better observe the interactions of the substances he ingested in his experiments!

As far as his tea discovery goes, one day, as he was boiling some water for another one of his experiments, some leaves from a nearby tree blew into it and, instead of plucking them out, he decided to let them stay and see how they tasted. Imagine his surprise and delight when, instead of the usual noxious herbal brew he had to gag down every day, he was able to taste the wonderfully delicious tea and experience its mildly stimulating effect.

Apparently he knew he was on to something and from then on he enjoyed a cup or bowl, as was used at the time. Imagine that after a long day swallowing, chewing and otherwise experimenting on himself with various leaves, powders and mixtures of everything from plants to fossilized bones (called Dragon Bones in Chinese medicine) to ground-up earthworms and scorpions, he was able to relax and enjoy a delicious and satisfying bowl of tea. Some texts even mention that Shen Nong then used this new brew to treat the after-effects of ingesting all the poisonous substances he was studying.

The other story of the origin of tea, which is even more fantastical, is about the great Indian Buddhist master, Bodhidharma or, as he is known in China, Da Mo. He is usually painted as a very serious character with great jutting eyebrows and a grim look on his face. Apparently, as the following story shows, he was quite a serious fellow.

It is said that at the age of 64 he undertook the long journey from India to China to share with the inhabitants of the Middle Kingdom his new teachings on Buddhism. His form of Buddhism was primarily centered on sitting meditation, called Chan. Later on this type of practice migrated to Japan where it was taken up by the Samurai class and called by its Japanese name, Zen.

Da Mo arrived in China in about 520 CE and went straight to see the emperor, who, he had been told, was a devout Buddhist. This emperor, named Wu, had indeed been a devout follower of Buddhism for some time and had erected many fine Buddhist temples, which he was very proud of. When Da Mo, with his fierce gaze, was brought into his August Presence, Emperor Wu was very excited. Here, at last, was a bonafide Buddhist master from India. He could not wait to meet him.

Da Mo strode into the royal reception hall and bowed to the emperor, seated upon the Dragon Throne. The emperor immodestly began listing all the temples he had built and all the ceremonies and rites he had paid for, thinking that the foreign master would be greatly impressed by his devotion. But Da Mo just stood there, staring at the emperor with his great dark eyes under their shocking eyebrows.

At last the emperor asked him how much merit he thought he had accumulated through all these good works.

"None whatsoever" came the short reply.

Surprised at this answer the emperor then decided to test this formidable teacher and asked, "What is the fundamental teaching of Buddhism?"

"Vast emptiness" was the reply.

The emperor was beginning to get hot under his richly brocaded collar. Who did this ragged monk think he was? "Just who do you think you are?" he thundered.

"I have no idea," said the monk and immediately turned about and strode out of the hall.

The emperor was incensed at this display of arrogance and audacity and he immediately proclaimed that this monk of ill repute was to have no privileges in any of the surrounding temples and monasteries. Of course this bothered Da Mo not at all. Instead he went to a cave up in the mountains outside the capital and entered into deep meditation, some say for the next nine years.

Now we come to the part about tea. It seems that during his long meditation sessions Da Mo kept having the highly irritating experience of his eyelids drooping. One day, in a fit of temper at this irksome habit, he ripped his eyelids off and threw them onto the ground outside the cave!

Later on, a bush grew from the place where his eyelids had fallen and for some reason some of his students decided to brew the leaves of the bush and found that it was very pleasant to taste and seemed to have the benefit of keeping them more awake and alert during the long hours of meditation they practiced.

Da Mo then went on to introduce his unique teachings of Buddhism and, because the monks at the temple he visited after his long meditation were so out of shape, he taught them exercises modeled after animal movements which eventually became what is now known as Shaolin Gong Fu.

However the tea plant came into being in China, tea quickly caught on as the hot beverage of choice, along with wine, which is often heated as well. But that is another story.

The first mention of the art of cultivating tea is found in the dictionary called the *Erh Ya*, which was originally written in the eighteenth century BCE. In the updated version by Kuo Po, written in 350 CE, he mentions tea leaves that were prepared by boiling them in water. This is very different from today's way of preparing tea, which is primarily by steeping the leaves for a short time.

Another ancient work is the *History of Huayang* by Chang Chu. This work tells us that tea was part of the tribute to the Zhou emperor Wu back in the eleventh century BCE. Later on, in the Han dynasty, a scholar named Yang Hiung, who lived from 53 BCE to 10 CE, wrote a dictionary called the *Fang Yen*, where he writes that tea was used at that point in history by people in Szechwan and Yunnan provinces. To this day, both of these areas are still heavily involved in tea growing and producing.

In the beginning then, tea was mostly drunk for its medicinal purposes rather than aesthetic or scholarly pursuit as in later Chinese history. At this time tea was used to treat digestive disorders (remember Shen Nong treating himself for self-poisoning) and also disorders of the nervous system. As previously mentioned, tea leaves were boiled and sometimes ingredients such as onions, ginger and orange were also added, which ended up creating quite a different brew than we are used to today.

Another group that got involved with tea was the Daoists. In their quest for immortality and enhanced energy, tea became part of their alchemical pursuits. As Beatrice Hohenegger tells us:

> When the first healers discovered tea, they marveled at the multitude of benefits this magical plant appeared to offer. It kept them alert, it healed their wounds, it was an invaluable food complement, and it was a beverage safer than water. Tea was so universally good, for the body's energy and vitality and also for the spirit, that Taoist alchemists believed they had found the answer to their search. Tea became their ingredient for eternal life.[2]

Tea culture develops in China

The culture of tea developed very slowly in China but by the Tang dynasty (618–907 CE) "tea came into being and took its place side by side with painting, calligraphy, poetic composition, lute-playing, *wei-chi* (a kind of chess played with 360 pieces), the martial arts, incense appreciation parties, landscape gardening and other scholarly pastimes."[3]

In those days tea was still primarily drunk after boiling the leaves. Tea was transported as hard bricks, which lasted a long time and were easy to carry from place to place. A piece of this very hard brick was broken off and then the tea was placed into boiling water, sometimes with added ingredients (as mentioned earlier).

Tea also became very popular with the nomads such as the Tibetans, the Mongolians and, Tartar and Turkish tribes who lived on the edges of the frontier. Since they had very little in the way of vegetables in their mostly meat diet, tea, boiled with yak milk and other ingredients, became a staple of their diet. It became so valuable to the nomads that the Chinese were able to control them to an extent by sending loads of tea to them. Indeed, the Chinese were often able to trade for horses, which the nomads had plenty of and which the Chinese always needed.

A whole system of tea as money was created just for this kind of trade. The tea that was sent north to the Tibetans and Mongolians was a cheap grade of tea compressed into very hard bricks, which could be stored for a very long time. This tea was sent to the "northern barbarians" via humans, donkeys or camels. These tribal people had no use for paper money or coins and so tea became a sort of currency in itself. And the great thing about it was that, unlike paper money or coins, which lessened in value the further away from the capital it got, this tea money actually become more valuable the further it traveled.

For the people who lived at very high altitudes like Tibet, where it was impossible to grow vegetables, tea became an important part of their diet. Mixed with yak butter (often fermented) and salt, it balanced their diet of mostly meat and barley flour. The custom was (and still is) to mix some roasted barley flour with the tea, making a sort of paste, which is then eaten. This is called *tsampa*, still eaten by nomadic herders in Tibet.

Another way in which tea became very important was as tribute to the emperor. Whole plantations were grown just to supply the royal court with the best tea. This custom remained in force all the way through the Qing dynasty (1644–1911 CE).

The best tea was called the "first pick in spring." This consisted of the first two leaves and bud only. John Blofeld's excellent book *The Chinese Art of Tea* gives us the following description of what it took to pick, process and deliver the emperor's tribute tea.

> By the end of the eighth century 30,000 people were involved in picking and firing tribute tea during a period of thirty days each year. Selecting the lucky day in the third moon (approximately April), tea officials assembled in a temple on the slopes of Mount Ming-Ling

and made sacrifices to the mountain deity. Thereafter a whole army of tea pickers, mostly girls, would be sent up the slopes in the early mornings, their movements controlled by red signal flags. Picking stopped at noon. During the remainder of each day the leaves would be fired, in other words dried in a special roaster, then powdered and pressed into a paste which would be put into moulds and kept there till it hardened into a cake before being packaged and sent off. This processing had to be completed by sunset.[4]

This custom of sending tribute tea to the emperor eventually got out of hand and ended up taking a huge amount of time out of the farmers' lives, who, instead of tending to their crops, ended up having to take a month off right at the beginning of planting time to harvest and process the emperor's tea. The sale of private tea was forbidden so the farmers could not make any money of their own. Much of what they were paid for working on the tribute tea they ended up spending in the encampments at the edge of the tea plantations, replete with brothels and wine shops.

Lu Yu's book of tea

It was also in the Tang dynasty that the first and most famous book on tea was written. This work, called the *Cha Jing* or *Tea Classic*, was written by a man called Lu Yu, who had quite a history of his own. Abandoned by his parents for an unknown reason and left by the side of the river when he was a young boy, he was, fortunately for him, discovered and adopted by the abbot of the nearby Chan Dragon Cloud Monastery. The abbot's name was Chin Chan and he raised the young lad and gave him the name Lu Yu. This he took from the *Book of Changes* or the *Yijing* (*I Ching*), an ancient book of divination and self-cultivation.

And so the boy was raised in the strict world of Chan Buddhism, the forerunner of the Japanese Zen. But apparently the lad did not appreciate the religious teachings of his father but felt more drawn to the world of Confucius, or Kong Fu Zi.

At one point, in exasperation at his behavior, Chin Chan put the boy to work cleaning the monastery's lavatories, which, as anyone could guess, can be a pretty disgusting job. Then he was put to tend the small herd of cattle that someone had given to the monastery, hoping to accumulate merit by saving their lives. The story is told about Lu Yu being so dedicated to his Confucian studies that he would ride the back of an ox, while practicing calligraphy on its neck! Eventually young Lu Yu had enough of the religious life and ran away with some traveling actors. With them he was trained in music and poetry and he excelled producing the plays.

But his great love was tea. He became an expert on tea and, after attaining a post in the government, was able to spend many years on his writings, including producing the first classic work on tea, a book in three volumes. Chapters covered such subjects as the mythological origins of tea in China; tools for picking, steaming, pressing, drying and storage of tea leaves and cake; the recommended procedures for the production of tea cake; twenty-eight items used in the brewing and drinking of tea; and the guidelines for the proper preparation of tea as well as various properties of tea, the history of tea drinking and the various types of tea known in fifth century China.

It was this work which made him famous enough to be noticed by the emperor who, being a bit of a tea aficionado himself, invited Lu Yu to the capital. There he gathered many students and disciples and became known as a tea master.

Lu Yu returned to the Dragon Cloud Monastery for a second time. While he was there he greatly impressed his adopted father with his mastery of tea. When Lu Yu left the monastery for the second time, Chin Chan decided that he would no longer drink tea, since any tea that had not been made by his son's hand was not fit to drink.

The emperor, having heard of this, decided to test the old man. He invited Chin Chan to the capital and offered him some tea that had been made by one of the ladies of the court, who was said to be quite an expert in the art of tea. The old monk, out of respect to the emperor, tried some of the tea but quickly put it down, apologizing that it was just not the same as the tea he had drunk that had been made by Lu Yu.

What Chin Chan did not know is that the emperor had asked Lu Yu to come to court and prepare some tea in secret in order to test the old monk's palate. "Surely," he thought to himself, "he cannot be as sensitive as he was making out to be." But, upon tasting the tea that had been secretly made by his son, Chin Chan cried out, "In truth, my Lord, this tea is so good that it cannot be any better if my son himself had prepared it!" The emperor decided that the old man was indeed as discerning as he said he was and brought Lu Yu out of hiding, to his adopted father's great surprise and joy.

Lu Yu's book describes everything from the plant itself, the tools for the manufacture of tea, the utensils used for tea preparation, the best kind of water used, as well as some tea history. He goes into great detail about everything. The following is his advice on the water for tea, which became a great subject of tea masters, many of whom claimed to be able to taste not only where the tea came from but also where the water used to prepare the tea came from!

> On the question of what water to use, I would suggest that tea made from mountain streams is best, river water is all right, but well-water tea is quite inferior. Water from the slow-moving streams, the stone-lined pools or mild-pure springs is the best of mountain water. Never

take tea made from water that falls in cascades, gushes from spring, rushes in a torrent or that eddies and surges as if nature were rinsing its mouth. Over usage of all such water to make tea will lead to illness of the throat.[5]

Here is a famous story of Lu Yu and his amazing powers concerning water:

Once when he was on a trip on a river with a local dignitary he was given water from midstream to taste. The extremely self-important dignitary handed Lu Yu a ladle, saying, "Here, Master, is the water which all men know as 'the finest under heaven.'" Upon tasting it Lu Yu frowned and said that the water was not from midstream but from closer to the shore where the water was not as pure.

"But that cannot be," said his host. "I am sure it was taken from midstream. I ordered it so myself."

"Perhaps," conceded the master, "but there is some other kind of water mixed into it, perhaps from another part of the river."

Later it was discovered that some of the water from the container had been lost when the boat had rocked and the servant had replaced it with water taken from nearer the shore.[6]

What I find most interesting is, after going into meticulous detail about what utensils are to be used for preparing tea, at the end of his book he lists all the reasons why one is allowed to dispense with them and just enjoy the tea. The reasons he gives are things like suddenly coming across a clear stream or fast-running brook, or if there are only five or fewer guests or if one is hiking up a mountain side, or if one simply wants to carry all the implements in a fruit basket and does not have the space for all of them.

This is a great example of the Daoist principle of not letting too strict a form get in the way of true enjoyment and deeply experiencing the inner truth of any teaching. Of course Lu Yu was more a follower of Confucius than Laozi, and I cannot help but think that his early years among the Chan Buddhists, which were heavily affected by Daoism, had some influence on his thinking.

Lu Yu gives a detailed description of the perfect tea leaves in the following passage from his classic work:

> Tea has a myriad of shapes. If I may speak vulgarly and rashly, tea may shrink and crinkle like a Mongol's boots. Or it may look like the dewlap of a wild ox, some sharp, some curling as the eaves of a house. It can look like mushrooms in whirling flight just as clouds do when they float out from behind a mountain peak. Its leaves can swell and leap as if they were being lightly tossed on the wind-disturbed water. Others will look like clay, soft and malleable, prepared for the hand of the potter and will be as clear and pure as if filleted through wood. Still others will twist and turn like the rivulets carved out by a violent rain in newly tilled fields. Those are the very finest of teas.[7]

Lu Yu made other important contributions to the art of tea. He wrote about serving and drinking tea as a practice to abide in the present moment, something he undoubtedly picked up in his days at the Dragon Cloud Monastery.

> Tea drinkers were encouraged to develop a spiritual appreciation for the everyday moments

in life as they performed the rituals of tea preparation. Lu Yu emphasized that all moments in life be attended with beauty—a concept that was to become central to the pleasure of tea drinking.[8]

The further development of tea in China

In the beginning tea was valued more for its medicinal properties than for the sheer enjoyment of drinking it. But by the Tang dynasty, considered by many to be the golden age of Chinese culture, it was drunk more for enjoyment than health. In those times tea became very popular with the nobility. Tea was still manufactured into cakes. Small shavings would be cut off the cake and then boiled, along with other ingredients, such as ginger, orange peel, cloves and peppermint or even fruit extracts and flowers.

The Tang dynasty was also when tea ware first became popular. Before this there were no special utensils for use in tea drinking. Lu Yu popularized the production and use of ceramic teacups, teapots and tea bowls.

In the Song dynasty (960–1279) the production of tea made it possible to create a more finely powdered tea. It was in the Song dynasty that people began grinding dried leaves into a powder and then adding boiling water. The mixture was then stirred with a bamboo whisk (much as it is still done in Japan for a tea ceremony) into a light, frothy drink. Contests would be held as to who could whip their tea into the best froth.

Tea tasting parties, where the participants had to guess what kinds of tea they were being served and where it came from, were important events. In *All the Tea in China*, we read:

> Among the wealthy, tea drinking as an art rose to new heights, and a small teahouse was included in many of the beautiful gardens that

41

officials built. The first Song emperor received
brick tea in gold boxes as tribute and Hui
Zong (r.1100–1125), its last to function fully,
wrote an exhaustive treatise on Song tea. He
was patron of a search that found several new
varieties.[9]

Unfortunately for Hui Zong, while he was paying so much
attention to his great love of tea and to a famous courtesan named
Li Shishi, the country was going to rack and ruin with several
large peasant uprisings. He was eventually forced to abdicate in
favor of his son. And then, Tartars from the north invaded China
and carried them both off as prisoners, where they remained for
the rest of their short lives.

It was in the Ming dynasty (1368–1644) that tea drinkers
began steeping leaves in hot water, as much of the world does
today. People stopped adding onions and other ingredients to
the tea and just drank it straight. Then again, the people of the
Ming dynasty had a passion for flowers and aromatic blossoms
and developed a way of adding them to the tea, creating such
historic brews as jasmine and osmanthus tea.

During these historic times it was the wealthy and educated
people who were able to enjoy all this tea. The simple farmers
and laborers had to settle for what is called, even today, country
people's tea, which is simply a cup or bowl of hot water.

One account from a tea connoisseur of the Ming dynasty is
from the book *Return to Dragon Mountain* by Jonathan D. Spence
and describes to what lengths tea lovers were willing to go:

> Zhang Dai's worldy-wise third uncle shared his
> highly developed taste with his nephew, and
> between them they explored a wide range of
> possibilities, checking which tea from which
> celebrated region went best with certain kinds
> of water. Their final conclusion was that the

spring water from the Speckled Bamboo Shrine, when allowed to sit for a recommended three days, brought out the richest aromas from the choicest leaves, and that when it was prepared in the finest of white porcelain, the color of the brew—the purest and palest of greens—was incomparable. The two men debated whether to add a petal or two of jasmine to the leaves, and agreed that adding the freshly boiled water to a little of the same water that had been allowed to cool in the same pot was the perfect method: watching the leaves stretch and unfold was like "seeing one hundred white orchid flowers open their petals in a wave of snow," and so it was that they named their discovery Snow Orchid tea.[10]

However, the world of tea was apparently a dog eat dog world back then and things went from bad to worse.

Within five years, by 1620 or so, this tea that Zhang and his uncle had named Snow Orchid had ousted its rivals from the connoisseurs' circles. But it was not long before unscrupulous businessmen began to market inferior teas under the Snow Orchid brand name, and those who drank it seemed not to know they were being gulled. A short time later, even the water course itself was lost. First, entrepreneurs from Shaoxing tried to use the water for wine making or else opened tea shops right by the spring itself. Next, a greedy local official tried to monopolize the spring's water for his own use and sealed it off for a while. But that increased the spring's reputation to such an extent that rowdy crowds began to gather at the shrine, demanding food, firewood and other handouts from the monks there and then brawling when they were refused. At last, to regain their earlier tranquility, the monks polluted the spring by filling it with manure, rotting bamboo and the overflow from their own drains. Three times Zhang Dai came with his household attendants to try to clear the spring, and three times the monks polluted it as soon as he had departed. Finally he gave up, though noting with sardonic amusement that many ordinary people, still remembering the magic of the old name, continued to brew their tea from the utterly contaminated Speckled Bamboo Shrine water and declared it fine.[11]

It was during China's last dynasty, the Qing (1644–1911), when China was invaded and conquered by a northern tribe called the Manchu, that the West discovered the joys of tea. It became so popular that England ended up with a huge trade deficit with China. Although tea had become an important part of English culture and something that the English could not live without, the Chinese had no interest in English goods. They would settle only for payment in silver.

Eventually English people became desperate to come up with something that the Chinese would be willing to pay for. They finally settled on opium. Chinese people had been using opium for some time already, mostly medicinally. Also, it was too expensive for the average person to afford enough to become addicted to. The English began flooding cheap opium, which they grew in their colonies in India; so many Chinese became addicted that the trade deficit starting leaning over to the English. Other European countries as well as American companies became fabulously wealthy with their opium business.

In China so many people became crippled by their addiction that the emperor decided to ban the sale of opium in China. He sent Commissioner Lin to Canton where most of the Western ships offloaded their opium, to enforce his edict. Commissioner Lin destroyed so much opium that the Western powers were furious and decided to teach the Chinese a lesson: thus began the first Opium War.

The Western powers, with their superior fire power, defeated the Chinese with almost no resistance. China was forced to sign a humiliating treaty ceding the island of Hong Kong to the English as well as opening four more ports. It was also forced to pay a huge indemnity to England. Eventually both France and the United States were able to draw up similar treaties. A second Opium War followed the first a short time later, with similar results.

It seems a great tragedy that the love of this glorious substance of tea should end up causing so much pain and humiliation to China. Fortunately, those days are over and China once again is a sovereign nation and is able to export vast amounts of tea to the rest of the world, though much of the tea drunk in the West, which is mostly black tea, is grown in India.

Notes

1.   Beatrice Hohenegger (2006) *Liquid Jade*, p.4.
2.   Ibid., p.11.
3.   Blofeld, *The Chinese Art of Tea*, p.2.
4.   Ibid., p.7.
5.   Lu Yu, *The Classic of Tea*, p.105.
6.   Solala Towler (2005) *Tales from the Tao*, p.220.
7.   Lu Yu, *The Classic of Tea*, p.70.
8.   Mary Lou Heiss and Robert J. Heiss (2007) *The Story of Tea*, p.10.
9.   Kit Chow and Ione Kramer (1990) *All the Tea in China*, p.10.
10. Jonathan D. Spence (2007) *Return to Dragon Mountain*, p.18.
11. Ibid., p.19.

3

Lu Meets a True Tea Master

Lu Yu was famous in Chang An (now Xian) as the Master of the Way of Tea. He had been working on his masterpiece, his treatise about tea, for some time and was almost finished. In it he listed all the most important aspects of the Way of Tea—from describing the different sorts of tea, what utensils to use and how to prepare it —even what type of water to use. He had been working very hard lately and when his friends came by one morning, inviting him on a picnic in the country, he had put his brushes and paper away with a sigh and joined them happily.

They had hiked up into the mountains on the outskirts of the city, reciting poetry to each other at the top of their voices, and Lu Yu had laughed as he had not for some time. They stopped halfway up the mountain and sat and had their meal, a simple affair, with a bit of wine. Lu Yu had not even brought his tea things with him, so relieved was he to have a break from his work.

His friends decided to take a nap after lunch and so Lu Yu, thrilled to be away from the confines of his studio, hiked a bit more by himself. He had gone some way, sniffing the pure air and reveling in the soft breezes of the countryside, when he noticed a small path off to the side of the main trail. It was very faint and he would not have seen it if he had not stopped to relieve himself nearby. He decided to follow it and see where it went.

After about half an hour of walking, and when he had almost decided to give up and rejoin his friends, he came upon a dilapidated hut. Actually it was not so much of a hut as a pile of raw lumber laid haphazardly together, its grass roof bald in places, so that surely the rain found its way through. Yet, strangely enough, there seemed to be such an air of peacefulness about it that Lu Yu decided to take a peek inside before setting off again.

To his great surprise there was a man sitting in the hut; at first glance he seemed as strange as the hut itself. His hair was long and uncombed, as was his long bushy beard. It looked so bushy that Lu Yu was half expecting a nest of birds to peep out at him. He must be some kind of recluse, thought Lu Yu to himself, although he did not wear his hair in a topknot as did the Daoists, nor was it shaved as with the Buddhists.

The strange man just sat there and stared at Lu Yu with a very mild expression but said nothing. Lu Yu bowed quickly and began to move away when the man seemed to come out of his trance and jumped up, exclaiming, "Good sir, please come in. I was just about to make some tea."

At the mention of tea, Lu Yu stopped himself. Perhaps it would be interesting to have tea with this rustic. It may be that the experience would provide some material for his book. If nothing else, it would make for an amusing story to his city friends when he rejoined them. So he bowed again and introduced himself.

"I am Lu Yu and I would very much like to have a bowl of tea with you," he said.

"Aha," said the man, "I would introduce myself by my good name but I am afraid that I have been too long in the mountains and have forgotten it! You may address me as Master of Simplicity, though I hardly deserve the name. I am afraid that this old gourd head of mine," and here he gave his head a resounding knock, "is too full of jumbled thoughts and ideas that swirl all around in it like a tide pool to be addressed as anything really but Master of Complications!" And here he gave such a deep laugh, straight from his belly, that Lu Yu could not help but join in.

"I'm sure it is not as bad as you say," he said.

But the man laughed again and said, "Oh but it is and even worse! But I do like to drink tea in the afternoon and would be honored if you would join me in my humble abode and share a bowl of rather inferior tea with me." Then he laughed again and Lu Yu joined in.

The Master of Simplicity then turned to the fire, which was blazing merrily along under a pot of water. He invited Lu Yu to sit in the place of honor and plopped himself down beside him.

"Please good sir," he said, "my tea is not very good but the water I have gathered is from a special spring high in the mountains that only I know about. It does impart a very special taste to the tea."

Here Lu Yu's ears picked up. He had just finished a section of his book on the best kind of water to be used for tea. He had listed all the best types of water as well as the types not to be used. He had said that water from freely flowing mountain streams was best and so was excited to learn that this is what was bubbling away in front of him.

The Master of Simplicity took the water off the fire and laid it aside. "It needs to cool down just a bit right now," he said to Lu Yu. "It has danced enough and now needs to rest before it can begin its work on the tea leaves." So saying, he got up and left the hut and went outside where he grabbed a handful of long grass and tied his great bushy hair back. He even combed his fingers through his beard, all the while smiling at Lu Yu in such a sweet way that Lu Yu felt his heart warm towards this strange fellow and Lu Yu found himself smiling right back. Even if the tea is bad, he thought to himself, I am having such an enjoyable time with this strange fellow that it will be worth gagging down whatever outlandish brew he serves me.

The Master of Simplicity came back into the hut, sat down, reached over behind himself and pulled out a simple bamboo container and popped off the lid. "This tea," he said, "is not very good but it does come from a very old tea tree. I had to climb quite a way up it to get the leaves from the very top. I almost fell off right onto my thick gourd head," he said laughing.

He handed the container of tea to Lu Yu, who, upon smelling it, was surprised at its fragrance. Perhaps this tea will not be so bad, he thought.

The man was looking at Lu Yu in a funny yet friendly way and Lu Yu thought he heard him mutter something to himself as he carefully shook out a small amount of leaves into his hand. He then raised his hand and held the leaves out in front of him. He muttered something again, very low yet very musical. "I am thanking the god of tea," he said to Lu Yu, "for showing me the way to the ancient tea tree and for allowing me to gather these leaves and for helping me not to fall on my head!" This time Lu Yu burst into laughter even before the Master of Simplicity did.

His name, thought Lu Yu to himself, sounds like that of a Daoist recluse. Perhaps he is one of those rare Daoist hermits who have shaken the dust of the world off his shoes and gone to live a life of "free and easy wandering." Though most of the Daoists that Lu Yu had met in the capital had been much more serious and even austere. I suppose it could be, thought Lu Yu, that he is just an eccentric who prefers spending his time in the mountains to living in the crowded city below.

The Master of Simplicity shook out a small handful of the tea leaves and placed them into a small clay pot that stood by the side of the fire. "Now," he said, turning to Lu Yu, "we have to perform the marriage of tea leaves and water." He then lifted the pot of hot water, no longer dancing, and poured it very slowly into the pot with the leaves.

"We have to go slowly," he said, "so that the water and the tea leaves can greet each other properly."

Lu Yu had never heard anyone talk about tea in this way. The tea aficionados that he spent time with were mostly very serious about their tea drinking. True, sometimes they composed poetry and once in a great while someone told a joke but mostly everyone took the tea ceremony very seriously. They were all so involved with being at one with the tea that they sometimes lost track of why they were actually there, to enjoy drinking tea!

As Lu Yu watched this tea master crooning to the pot of tea, he remembered the excitement with which he had first greeted the Way of Tea. As a boy he had been left on a riverbank where he had been found by Chin Chan, the abbot of the local Chan Buddhist temple. Though he had been raised there, he often found the Buddhist rites practiced to be tedious and uninteresting.

But his adoptive father had introduced him to the Way of Tea and that was something that he would always be grateful for. He remembered how, at a certain time of day, his adoptive father would invite him to sit with him in front of a scroll painting of a gentle landscape or of the Goddess of Mercy, Kuan Yin, and together they would share a bowl of tea. Chin Chan's tea ceremony was very simple. He would just heat water in one pot, take up the brick of dried tea leaves that sat on a shelf in a place of honor and drop tea leaves in to boil for just a few moments.

"The Way of Tea is very simple, my son," he would say. "It is only to boil water, along with tea leaves and drink it. Anything else is superfluous."

Those memories of his time with his adoptive father, drinking tea and talking of this and that, was what Lu Yu carried with him when he fled the temple at an early age to join the traveling players he had met one day in town.

Now he was the most famous tea master in the Middle Kingdom. It was the days of the "glorious Tang dynasty" and art and culture in China was reaching new heights. And now Lu Yu was working on the definitive treatise on the Way of Tea. Many tea masters were eagerly awaiting this work and Lu Yu was sure that his name would go down in history as the tea master of tea masters (as well it did). But now sitting here in this hut with this rustic fellow and about to drink some local tea made him more excited and happy than he had been for some time.

"This tea that we are about to drink," said the Master of Simplicity, "comes about through the marriage of not only the boiling water and the tea leaves but actually through the union of Heaven—which bestows the rain and sunlight on the tea tree and that of the Earth—which gives of itself so that the tea tree may grow tall and strong. It is in this way that this simple bowl of tea represents all of Heaven and all of Earth."

"Actually," added the Master of Simplicity, "that is rather a lot for one simple bowl of tea to have to carry." And here he laughed his jolly belly laugh again.

The Master of Simplicity had put the clay pot over the coals of the fire and allowed it to come to a very gentle boil. Lu Yu noticed that he had not added anything else to the brew. Lu Yu's friends in the city were used to adding all sorts of things to their tea—such ingredients as ginger, orange peel or even small onions. Also, Lu Yu was used to drinking his tea from exquisite porcelain bowls. He had friends in the capital who even drank from vessels made from gold and silver, though Lu Yu disliked using anything metal when brewing and drinking tea. But here the man was pouring the tea into several very wobbly wooden bowls.

Lu Yu stretched out his hand and took his bowl of tea from his strange new friend. He held it up in front of him and gazed into the bowl, noticing the deep, rich color of the tea. It was true that a few errant wisps of straw had alighted on the surface of the tea, no doubt falling from the dilapidated roof, but he quickly pulled them out. Next he held the bowl up to his nose and inhaled deeply. Ah, he thought, this is really very good tea. It has an earthy smell, which was good, but it also had an indefinable odor or freshness. It was almost as though he could smell the light on the leaves as it grew high in its mountain valley.

Next he raised the bowl to his lips and took a small sip, being careful because it was very hot and also so that he could properly appreciate its flavor. Amazingly, it was wonderful! He tried another sip and then another. It was simply some of the best tea that he had ever tasted. Because of his educated and experienced palate he could taste the purity of the water that had been used to brew it. It had a slight mineral flavor but that was good. It was part of what gave the tea its health-enhancing qualities. The taste was both rich and light. And the taste of the wooden lip of the bowl also seemed to give it an earthy flavor.

He looked around himself, both at his strange yet gracious host, who was lost in his own moment of tea, and at his surroundings. He had never, in his life, been in such a dilapidated and rustic building before. Yet he felt strangely comfortable there, sitting on an old straw mat by this small fire with his newfound tea friend.

Lu Yu felt himself smiling and he noticed that the Master of Simplicity was smiling into his bowl of tea. "This tea," he said slowly, "reminds me of my home, far away from here. To me it tastes of the sun, the wind, and the earth. It tastes of rain, of dew and of the rock that ran beneath the water. It reminds me of my past yet seems to lure me gently into my future." And here he sighed deeply and looked over at Lu Yu. "Truly," he said, "this little bowl of tea has so much to say to me that I could spend all afternoon listening to it." Then he looked up and laughed, "But what I think I will do is drink it," and here he lifted his bowl to his lips and drank the last of the tea in it.

Both of the men fell silent then and spent a little time each in his own world, while the sun floated over the roof of the hut. Lu Yu suddenly realized that he had been gone for some time and his friends were probably wondering what had happened to him. He got up and bowed to the Master of Simplicity, saying, "I thank you for a wonderful bowl of tea and for the deep pleasure I have found in your company."

The Master of Simplicity then got up and bowed deeply to Lu Yu. "I too thank you," he said, "for sharing with me this simple brew. Perhaps we will meet again one day and can enjoy this wonderful marriage of Heaven and Earth again." And here he laughed and began gathering his few tea things and putting them into a frayed basket.

Later on Lu Yu could not remember leaving the hut or walking back down the faint trail back to his friends. They were indeed worried about him and when he told them of his meeting with the Master of Simplicity and of the wonderful tea he had drunk with him, they wanted to run up the trail to meet this strange tea master but Lu Yu assured them that the Master of Simplicity would be long gone by now. And so they made their way back to the city.

Some time after that Lu Yu finished his treatise on tea, his *Cha Ching*. In it he listed all the tools for the proper brewing and enjoyment of tea, including the brazier, the stoker, the fire tongs, the basket, the rollers, the measure, the water ladle, the water filter, the water dispenser, among many other things. He listed the types of water to be used and the various elements of tea brewing itself.

But then, at the end, he added a strange postscript. After spending much time on the endless lists of things that were absolutely necessary for the proper preparation and drinking of tea he said at the end: "Concerning the proper equipment for brewing tea: If one finds himself among the pines and there is a rock on which to sit, he may omit the utensil rack."

He then went on to say that if using firewood then many of the other utensils may be eliminated. And if one finds a clear running brook, or one is climbing up a steep cliff, even more may be dispensed with. Smaller and smaller goes the list until only the bare essentials are listed. Some of his friends could not help but remark upon Lu Yu's afternoon with the Master of Simplicity and wondering if perhaps something of his experience there could not help but influence this urbane man of cultivation to the rustic pleasures of a simple bowl of tea in the bosom of nature.

4

Tea Mind, Zen Mind

The close affinity between Zen teachings and the
tea ceremony helped mold the rules and ritual in
the development of cha-no-yu, and the simplicity
and purity inherent in the religion influenced the
form of the tea ceremony. In effect, the same
harmony of mind, which could only be attained
upon entering the gate of a Zen temple, could
now be achieved in the serene atmosphere that
pervades the tea room.[1]

Tea seeds were first brought to Japan by a Zen priest named Eisai
Myo-an in 1191. He planted the seeds first in the Hizen district
and then transplanted them in Kakata, Kyushu, where the first
temple of his new sect, the Rinzai school, was built. It is said that
at one point the emperor stopped by the temple and was served
green tea and enjoyed it so much that he caused it to be planted
in five districts near Chang An.

At this time Eisai began to promote the use of powdered tea,
as tea was used in China at that time. China went on to the
steeping method that is used nowadays in China and much of
the rest of the world. But in Japan, at least in the tea ceremony,
powdered tea is still used.

At first the Japanese used tea for medicinal purposes and as a stimulant for long periods of meditation in the temples, much as Da Mo's first disciples had back in China.

Eisai wrote a small book on tea called *Kissa Yojoki* or *Tea Drinking is Good for Health*. In it he recommended drinking tea for treating five types of disease: loss of appetite, drinking water disease, paralysis, boils and beri-beri. This work did a lot for popularizing the use of tea across Japan.

It is in Japan that tea drinking and tea ceremony, which was heavily influenced by Zen Buddhism, became an elaborate part of the path to enlightenment.

> It constituted the mystical centre of the rites of withdrawel, self-abnegation and the attainment of nothingness in the new sects. To have its full effect, to release the maximum amount of caffeine and other relaxants and stimulants, tea had to be prepared and served in its purest and most powerful form. So it was ground into a powder and used as fresh as possible. It was also prepared and served in an almost sacred manner, emphasizing and encouraging the belief in its mystical power. So the whole elaborate tea ceremony developed. As an old Buddhist saying put it, the taste of *ch'an* (Zen) and the taste of *ch'a* (tea) are the same.[3]

In Japan the tea ceremony is known as *chanoyu* and (as quoted above) has been heavily influenced by Zen Buddhism. Zen Buddhism came to Japan from China, where it was known as Chan (Sitting), and was the form of Buddhist practice favored by Da Mo. This is a form of Buddhism that was greatly influenced by Daoism.

> The spirit of tea is the spirit of Zen; there is no
> "spirit of tea" independent of the spirit of Zen.
> If you do not know the taste of Zen, you do
> not know the taste of tea.[2]

For many people the most attractive elements of Zen practice are the non-reliance on scripture, the use of humor and paradox in teaching, the "being in the present moment" attitude, the earthy simplicity of mindful practice in daily life, and the simple yet profound practice of "just sitting."

But what many people do not realize is that all of these elements of Zen were taken from or evolved from Chinese Daoism. After all, Zen Buddhism is quite a different creature than the Buddhism that developed in India and the rest of Southeast Asia. It was in its travels and transformation from India to China to Japan that Indian Buddhism became what we know today as Zen.

The term *zazen*, from which the term *zen* comes, means simply to sit. It is a Japanese form of the Daoist practice *zuowanglun*, which is often translated as "sitting in oblivion" or "sitting and forgetting."

Perhaps the most famous of the Chinese patriarchs is Hui Neng, who followed the Daoist tradition of the "wise simpleton" described in the *Daodejing* as follows:

> Most people have more than they need.
> I alone possess nothing.
> Other people are brilliant
> While I know nothing.
> Other people are clear
> While I alone am muddled.
> I feel apart from them,
> Like a windy and stormy sea.

(Chapter 20)

The story of how Hui Neng became the sixth patriarch is a good one. Hui Neng worked in the monastery kitchen and was looked down upon by the other monks as being an illiterate rustic. When it came time for the fifth patriarch, Hung Jen, to pass on the mantle, he decided to hold a poetry contest to come up with his successor. So he gathered his students together and gave them instructions on writing a poem describing the experience of enlightenment.

Shen Hsiu, his senior student, duly wrote a poem on the wall leading into the meditation hall. He wrote:

> Our body is the bodhi tree,
> Our mind a mirror bright,
> Polish it diligently,
> Letting no dust alight.

This impressed all the other students and it seemed as though Shen Hsiu had a lock on the contest but Hung Jen was not so sure. Hui Neng, busy in the kitchen and serving the other monks their meals, heard their excited conversation about Shen Hsiu's poem. One night he had a sudden experience of illumination (later called *satori* in Japanese Zen) and came up with a poem of his own. Of course he could not write it out himself, being illiterate, but got one of the younger monks to write it out for him. His went like this:

> There is no bodhi tree,
> The mind is not a mirror bright.
> Since all is inherently empty,
> Where can dust alight?

When the fifth patriarch came upon this poem he realized that Hui Neng was the one he had been looking for. He also realized that this would not be a welcome outcome for the other monks, as they all believed Shen Hsiu was the rightful heir.

So, under the cover of nightfall, Hung Jen gave Hui Neng transmission of the Dharma of Sudden Enlightenment and the robe of office and sent him out on his own, to keep him safe from the angry monks, who were outraged at his choice for successor. From here Hui Neng went on to build what is now called the Southern School of Chan Buddhism.

Buddhism was introduced to Japan as early as 553 CE from Korea. Then, much later, Eisai Myo-an (1141–1215) founded what we know today as Zen. He was trained in China, studying at Mount Tien Tai, which is still known for its Buddhist masters. It was there that he is said to have achieved enlightenment (or what the Daoists would call "attaining Dao") and was made the official Japanese emissary of the true dharma of the Buddha.

Upon returning to Japan he founded Kennin-ji Monastery in Kyoto in 1202. Upon his death his disciple Myozen also went to China to study at Tien Tai, taking with him his student Dogen, who would go on to become one of the most influential Zen teachers in history.

Although space does not permit me to delve too deeply into the world of Zen, a few words here should provide a small sense of this enigmatic and influential philosopher. While there developed, over the centuries, quite a long and involved philosophy of Zen, the main emphasis down through the years has been on practice. In Zen the emphasis is on direct experience. By sitting *zazen* and, in the Rinzai school, grappling with Zen riddles or *koans*, the practitioner is forced to let go of any preconditioned mind sets or ego constructs and bore deeply into his or her own original mind or Buddha mind. This can free up an amazing amount of energy and spiritual insight. Also, by emphasizing everyday reality and such simple activities as sitting and walking, Zen practice can both deepen and enlarge such mundane activities and open one to direct perception of the truth. Shunryu Suzuki, one of the first teachers to bring Zen Buddhism to the West, says this about the practice of Zen:

> Zazen practice is the direct expression of our true nature. Strictly speaking, for a human being, there is no other practice than this practice; there is no other way of life than this way of life.[4]

And:

> We should find perfect existence through imperfect existence.[5]

One of my favorite stories concerning Zen people is from Sushila Blackman's fascinating book, *Graceful Exits: How Great Beings Die — Death Stories of Hindu, Tibetan Buddhist and Zen Masters*.

> As Master Tenno was dying, he called to his room the monk in charge of food and clothing in the temple. When the monk sat down by the bed, Master Tenno asked, "Do you understand?"
>
> "No," the monk replied.
>
> Tenno, picking up his pillow, hurled it through the window, and fell back dead.[6]

This story gives us a flavor of how tough and pragmatic the Zen path can be.

In his useful book, *Wabi Sabi: The Japanese Art of Impermanence*, Andrew Juniper says:

> The renowned monk Hakuin had a favorite expression that meditation in the midst of activity was far better than meditation in stillness. For the Zen monks, everything they undertook became a spiritual task in which they had to immerse themselves totally, and

in doing so they absorbed themselves in the
activity rather than in their ego's understanding
of the activity.[7]

And:

In Zen philosophy the mind should be a
window, rather than a mirror, so that the world
is seen directly and not through filters of the
intellect.[8]

Which brings us to the connection between Tea Mind and Zen
Mind.

The tea ceremony in Japan evolved into a much more austere
and often rigid ritual than is practiced in China. This has a lot to
do with the fact that Chan Buddhism, as it traveled to Japan from
China, was often taken up by the samurai class, who overlaid their
own sense of *bushido* (*bushi*—samurai, *do*—way) onto it. This was
a strict code of honor that these famous warriors lived by.

The emphasis in Zen practice is on still sitting and, to the
greatest extent possible, living in the present moment, uncluttered
with extraneous thoughts and concepts. There is a lot of talk in
the traditional Zen tales about its practitioners achieving sudden
enlightenment, though this is often after years of practice.
Sometimes it is when the practitioner is shaken out of their usual
sense of themselves by a sudden and often strange experience,
such as being hit on the head with the master's sandal.

One of my favorites is the one about the practitioner who,
after years of intense study and meditation, has gotten nowhere
and so decides to leave the temple and rejoin the world of dust.
He goes straight to a brothel and begins drinking and dancing
with the women there. Later that night, when answering the call
of nature in the outhouse, upon hearing the plopping sound his
stool makes as it falls into the outhouse hole, he is suddenly
awakened to his true Buddha nature!

Because of this often very ascetic way of training, the early practitioners of the Way of Tea were very strict as to how it all had to happen. It became a way for the participants in the tea ceremony to experience the transcendental reality of life itself. In *The Book of Tea*, the most famous tea classic of Japan, Kakuzo Okakura says:

> Tea with us became more an idealization of the form of drinking; it is a religion of the art of life. The beverage grew to be an excuse for the worship of purity and refinement, a sacred function at which the host and guest joined to produce for that occasion the utmost beatitude of the mundane.[9]

It has been said that the taste of Zen and the taste of tea are one and the same. "If you do not know the taste of Zen, you do not know that taste of tea."[10]

And lastly, Sen'o Tanaka says:

> In my opinion, although there is a very close relationship between the ethics of Zen and cha-no-yu, they differ in the following manner: While Zen calls for enlightenment of the individual through meditation and detachment, cha-no-yu is an art in which people communicate with each other through simplicity of spirit and purity of mind.[11]

The philosophy and practice of chanoyu evolved over time from its early beginnings in the 1200s to the time of the most famous tea master of Japan, Sen No Rikyu (1522–1591). He began studying the Way of Tea when he was a boy. His first teacher, Kitamuki Dochin, had taught him the Way of Tea in the old *shoin* style, which used a large reception room. Later, when he studied with another tea master, Jo-o, he was introduced to the simple style of the small thatched hut.

Rikyu studied Zen at the great Kaitoku-ji temple in Kyoto, a place that had a long relationship to the Way of Tea. There he learned to quieten his mind and to focus so completely on just one thing—whether it was his breathing or brewing tea—that he lost track of everything else and entered into a deep relationship with that moment. Nothing else mattered but that moment, that stillness of that moment, or the stillness in each moment. Thus he had brought a deep sense of awareness and reverence to his tea ceremony and earned great fame as a practitioner and as a teacher, first to the great Shogun Oda Nobunaga and then to his successor, Toyotomi Hideyoshi, who had unified all of Japan under one ruler for the first time.

His influence on the tea ceremony was huge. He discouraged the use of the expensive and fancy tea bowls from China and introduced the simple, rough *raku* bowls, fashioned by hand instead of on a wheel and not perfectly round. Instead of the luxurious glazes from China they were made with a rough deep red and black glaze, the better to show off the deep green of the tea.

He made other changes too. Instead of using the expensive porcelains of China for his tea utensils, he began using simple, natural utensils made of local wood or bamboo, the better to be in harmony with the Way of Tea and how it related to the Way of Zen.

Rikyu knew that many people who studied the Way of Tea never delved all the way into this simple yet sublime ritual. They mostly liked to show off their expensive tea utensils and liked to impress their guests with their arcane knowledge of the tea ceremony. But their tea ceremony lacked depth and maturity and the simple yet awesome power of the true Way of Tea.

For them he had written a famous poem:

> Though many people drink tea,
> If you do not truly know
> The Way of Tea,
> Tea will drink you up.

For the tea ceremony was not simply about drinking tea. It was about the art of life, of creating a perfect moment of peace and being at one with the tea, at one with the simple yet profound power of giving one's whole being to the ceremony, of investing one's whole attention to each unfolding moment. It was a ceremony that took the simple art of drinking tea to a sacred level, where the host and the guests shared a moment of worship of the simple art of preparing and drinking of tea together, elevating them to a level of purity and refinement. The Way of Tea and the Way of Zen were one and the same. It was in that deep reverence and fierce attention to the moment at hand that one was able to transcend the mundane world and travel to the deep heart of life, and reveling in a deep appreciation for the simple, unadorned reality that the Way of Tea encompassed.

Kakuzo Okakura describes this spirit in this way:

> Tea with us became more than an idealization of the form of drinking; it is a religion of the art of life. The beverage grew to be an excuse for the worship of purity and refinement, a sacred function at which the host and guest joined to produce for that occasion the utmost beatitude of the mundane. The tea-room was an oasis in the dreary waste of existence where we travelers could meet to drink from the common spring of art appreciation. The ceremony was an improvised spring of art appreciation. The ceremony was the improvised drama whose plot was woven about the tea, the flowers, and

the paintings. Not a color to disturb the tone of the room, not a sound to mar the rhythm of things, not a gesture to obtrude on the harmony, not a work to break the unity of the surroundings, all movements to be performed simply and naturally—such were the aims of the tea-ceremony. And strangely enough it was often successful.[12]

Here is a list of the seven tea rules, which Rikyu posted on the wall at a temple in Sakai:

When the guests have arrived at the waiting-lodge and all the like-minded participants are assembled there, the host announces himself by sounding a wooden gong.

As far as washing the hands is concerned, what really matters on this Way is the purification of the heart.

The host must approach the guests with every respect and conduct them to the tea-room. If the host is a person without composure and imagination, if the tea and utensils are of bad taste, and if the natural layout and planning of the trees and rocks in the tea-garden are unpleasing, then it is as well to go straight back home.

As soon as the boiling water sounds like the wind in the pine trees and the sound of a gong rings out, the guests enter the tea-room for a second time. It is unforgivable to let slip the right moment as regards water and fire.

Neither inside nor outside the tea-room let the conversation turn to worldly things: this is a commandment of old.

At a true gathering neither guest nor host has recourse to fine words or smooth airs.

A gathering may not exceed two double hours in length. If, however, this time is exceeded in the course of discussion of the Buddha's teachings and aesthetic matters, that is not objectionable.[13]

Unfortunately for Rikyu, he incurred the wrath of Hideyoshi and was ordered to commit ritual suicide or *seppeku* (see Chapter 7, One Last Cup). But his influence on the Way of Tea was immense. A great part of this was due to his deep sensitivity, which went beyond the confines of the tea ceremony itself. Probably because of his early training in Zen he brought the sensibility of Zen practice to the role of tea master. He once wrote:

It is said that the participants can tell by the sound of the footwear (on the stepping stones) whether the others are accomplished practitioners or not. The person who walks with equanimity and detachment, neither bustling in step, nor as stealing in, you should recognize as a master. One lacking in a genuine grasp of chanoyu, however, will be incapable of judging.[14]

Indeed, the tea master Sen Sotan (1578–1658), upon being asked to reveal the nature of *chanoyu*, answered that it was "the sound of windblown pines in a painting."[15]

There is a story about Hideyoshi and Rikyu, in one of the many times the lord tested his tea master, when he placed a large bronze bowl filled with water and put it in the place of honor in the tea-room. Beside it he placed a branch of plum blossoms and told Rikyu to make a flower arrangement out of it. This was, of course, some kind of test for Rikyu.

Traditionally the alcove was the most honored space in the teahouse. The teahouse itself had evolved over the years to become a very small, very simple space. A Zen priest named Murata Shuko (1422–1502) had created the formal teahouse that was used for centuries after. This consisted of a room containing four and a half tatami mats, which measures out to nine square yards (7.5m²). There was usually a fire pit in the center of the room, where the host prepared the tea. The entrance door was very short so that one had to bow and crawl into the room on hands and knees, which was thought to encourage a feeling of humbleness.

Kazuko Okakura describes the teahouse or tea-room like this:

> All our great tea-masters were students of Zen and attempted to introduce the spirit of Zenism into the actualities of life. Thus the room, like other equipments of the tea ceremony, reflects many of the doctrines. The size of an orthodox tea-room, which is four mats and a half, or ten feet square, is determined by a passage in the Sutra of Vikramadytia. In that interesting work, Vikramadytia welcomes the Saint Mansushiri and eighty-four thousand disciples of Buddha in a room of this size—an allegory based on the theory of the non-existence of space to the

truly enlightened. Again the roji, the garden path which leads from the machiai to the tea-room, signified the first stage of meditation—the passage into self-illumination. The roji was intended to break connection with the outside world, and to produce a fresh sensation conducive to the full enjoyment of aestheticism in the tea-room itself. ...One may be in the midst of a city, and yet feel as if he were in the forest far from the dust and din of civilization.[16]

To understand a little better just what the test was that Hideyoshi was presenting to Rikyu, we shall take a little closer look at the flower arrangement in a teahouse. Unlike *ikebana*, which uses elaborate flower arrangements, the tradition of flower arranging in a teahouse is called *chabana* and follows totally different rules than ikebana. In chabana flowers are arranged in a completely natural way, as if they are growing in a field. Only one or two flowers are used, unlike ikebana, which can use many flowers, leaves and stems; the stems can be artificially bent or even grown that way, much like *bonsai*.

The art of chabana requires a great deal of sensitivity from the tea master. The idea is to introduce the flowers in such a simple and natural state that the tea guests may be able to view and appreciate them for their simple natural beauty and not for any sort of artifice.

So what Hideyoshi was doing here was testing Rikyu's mastery of chabana. By giving him a bowl of water instead of a vase or piece of bamboo, and allowing him only one branch of plum blossoms to make a flower arrangement, he was sure he had put Rikyu in an impossible situation.

But what Rikyu did was hold the branch of plum blossoms over the bowl of water and gently shake the branch so that the petals floated downward on the surface of the water. In this way both the open blossoms as well as the buds floated together in a serene and elegant way. Rikyu had won again!

The reason I am going into such length about this ancient tea master is to be able to give you some feeling for what, to the Japanese, it means for someone to be a master of chanoyu. It is not just about being able to serve a good cup of tea or to be able to follow a ritual note for note. There was, and is, still room for individual expression even in the oftentimes extremely rigid ritual that comprises the Zen Way of Tea.

Perhaps the most important practice in the Zen tea ceremony is in the complete awareness of each moment as it unfolds and as well as a deep connection to each step of the ceremony. This teaching is reflected in the following instructions:

> If you are to take up the teascoop, immerse your heart and mind fully in it alone and give nothing whatever to other matters. This is to treat it first and last. When replacing it, do so conveying your heart and mind to it from their depths, as in the beginning. Such treatment is not restricted to the teascoop, it applies to all the implements that you handle.
>
> When, in putting down a utensil, you release it and withdraw your hand, do so without the slightest dismissing it from your awareness and shift the mind just as it is to the next utensil to be treated. Prepare tea as the forms (kata) prescribe, without relaxing the spirit at any point; this is called "performing in the continuity of spirit." It is wholly the functioning of chanoyu samadhi.[17]

This can, and should, also be practiced in whatever it is that one does. In this way, everyday activities can take on the depth of a truly Zen experience and allow each unfolding moment to contain the possibility of complete awareness.

Another interesting concept in Zen tradition is that of *wabi sabi*. According to Wikipedia,

> the word *wabi* connotes rustic simplicity, freshness or quietness, and can be applied to both natural and human-made objects, or understated elegance. It can also refer to quirks and anomalies arising from the process of construction, which add uniqueness and elegance to the object. *Sabi* is beauty or serenity that comes with age, when the life of the object and its impermanence are evidenced in its patina and wear, or in any visible repairs.[18]

Sabi can also mean a feeling of the sweetness of loneliness, of impermanence, of not having control over anything, or even the sweetness of suffering. These are very Japanese concepts and can be difficult for Westerners to understand. The huge popularity of the Sakura Festival, when Japanese people go out *en masse* to view the blossoming of the cherry trees, is a great example of this. The Japanese enjoy seeing the fragile beauty of the cherry blossoms, not only because they are beautiful in themselves, but also because they are not permanent. They bloom for only a short time and then are blown away on the wind.

Our own lives are also like this. We are here for only a short time, and then we are swept away like the cherry blossoms. For many people this is a source of great suffering but for the Japanese it is what imparts beauty and value to our lives. There is a sense of sweet suffering, a feeling of the delicate exquisiteness that our lives encompass. While the Chinese phrase *biku*, or "to eat bitter," means to be able to take the bitter as well as the sweet experiences in life, the Japanese term *wabi* connotes much more than just putting up with the bitter. Rather it is a deep appreciation for all that is transient and changeable. Or, as one of my Japanese friends says, wabi can also mean having compassion for what we cannot change.

Or, as Andrew Juniper says:

> Wabi Sabi embodies the Zen nihilistic cosmic view and seeks beauty in the imperfections found as all things, in a constant state of flux, evolve from nothing and devolve back to nothing.[19]

And:

> Wabi Sabi is an intuitive appreciation of a transient beauty in the physical world that reflects the irreversible flow of life in the spiritual world. It is an understated beauty that exists in the modest, rustic, imperfect, and even decayed, an aesthetic sensibility that finds a melancholy beauty in the impermanence of all things.[20]

It is with this aesthetic in mind that teahouses are traditionally built from very simple materials—old wood, bamboo, grasses. When a student of Rikyu asked him what kind of room was most appropriate for a tea ceremony he is said to have answered, "A room in which much old wood has been used for repairs."[21]

Wabi sabi, then, is an appreciation for wood that is weathered and old. It prefers the simple, earthy glazes and shapes of raku pottery over the exquisite Chinese porcelain that was used in the beginning of tea ceremony. It favors the utilitarian over the merely decorative. It likes things that are asymmetrical rather than perfectly symmetrical. It appreciates each fleeting moment for itself, not for what the future may or may not bring. It enjoys what we might call the simple things of life, not just despite, but *because* of, the fact that they are impermanent and changeable. It despises ostentation, showiness, the gaudy, the fancy and the complicated.

What drew the samurai class to the tea ceremony was the fact that it was a place of quiet serenity in the midst of their battle-filled lives. It was a place where they could let down their guard and enter into a timeless realm where the simple appreciation of a scroll painting, a piece of calligraphy or a simple flower arrangement was enough to fill a morning. It was where they could listen to the quiet bubbling of the tea water as it was brought to a gentle boil. It was an opportunity to observe the slow, simple and austere movements of the tea master.

In other words, it was a chance to leave the ordinary world of cause and effect and enter a world of precise and time-honored ceremony where the simple act of drinking a cup of tea would symbolize the entrance into a world of quiet and peace. And, in this way, if their lives were too busy or too violent for them to find time, with equanimity, to sit Zen, they could at least drink Zen.

By emphasizing the ordinary and mundane, Zen teachers constantly point the student back towards the beginning, to what is eternal and unchanging. The great meeting between Zen and the Way of Tea has produced many sublime examples of art, poetry and a way of life that has endured for over eight hundred years.

Notes

1. Sen'o Tanaka (1973) *The Tea Ceremony*, p.79. Copyright © Kodansha International Ltd., and Dai Nihon Chado Gakkai, 1973, 1998.
2. Dennis Hirota (1995) *Wind in the Pines*, p.269.
3. Alan Macfarlane and Iris Macfarlane (2004) *Green Gold: The Empire of Tea*, p.54.
4. Shunryu Suzuki (1970) *Zen Mind, Beginner's Mind*, p.19.
5. Ibid., p.98.
6. Sushila Blackman (2005) *Graceful Exits*, p.37.
7. Andrew Juniper (2003) *Wabi Sabi: The Japanese Art of Impermanence*, p.26.
8. Ibid., p.26.

9. Kakuzo Okakura (2001) *The Book of Tea*, p.31.
10. Hirota, *Wind in the Pines*, p.269.
11. Tanaka, *The Tea Ceremony*, p.79.
12. Okakura, *The Book of Tea*, p.31.
13. Macfarlane and Macfarlane, *Green Gold: The Empire of Tea*, p.58.
14. Hirota, *Wind in the Pines*, p.221.
15. Ibid., p.26.
16. Okakura, *The Book of Tea*, p.59.
17. Hirota, *Wind in the Pines*, p.24.
18. http://en.wikipedia.org/wiki/wabi-sabi, accessed 16 October, 2009.
19. Juniper, *Wabi Sabi*, p.1.
20. Ibid., p.51.
21. Hirota, *Wind in the Pines*, p.254.

5

Just One Flower

Toyotomi Hideyoshi had risen from very humble ranks through a combination of guile, cunning and great courage to become ruler of all of Japan. As a former low-level samurai he could be very fierce. Having been raised on the battlefields of Japan, Hideyoshi was a man of great strength, both of body as well as spirit. He always held himself erect and proud, like the great samurai warrior he was. But this fierce warrior was also a great lover of tea and tea ceremony. Like many samurai of his day, Hideyoshi felt the austere and formal tea ceremony not only gave him the space and time to relax and let down the many stresses of being a ruler but also gave him a window into another way of being, of what the monks called Zen Mind. In the teahouse he could become a humble tea drinker, at one with the ritual and with the eternal moment.

While he was not the actual emperor of Japan, he was the ruling regent, and had great power. He had once served tea to the emperor himself in a small teahouse inside the Imperial Palace. Once he had served tea to 803 people at a great tea ceremony held in Kyoto in 1587. He even had a tea pavilion built of gold that he could take with him when he traveled.

But Hideyoshi, at least partly, was still a humble man who had not forgotten his simple origins and spent a great deal of his time meditating in a small hut when he was not lavishly entertaining his many friends and political allies.

Rikyu was the most famous tea master of his time. His tea ceremony is said to have had great spiritual depth. It was he who had done away with the elaborate and costly tea bowls from China and Korea and had created the simple, rustic style of pottery called raku. He had brought a sense of Zen simplicity to the tea ceremony, using simple bamboo utensils and cutting to the very essence of Tea Mind.

At one point Hideyoshi had petitioned the emperor for permission to give Rikyu the title of *koji*, or "enlightened recluse," so that he might enter the Imperial Palace as Hideyoshi's special tutor. Thus Rikyu had risen to a very high social position. Some said that it was indeed too high.

Some said that the promotion had gone to Rikyu's head and he had become arrogant. Sometimes Hideyoshi tested his tutor, giving him difficult tasks that were supposed to humble the great tea master. But Rikyu always managed to handle them with ease. Hideyoshi was torn between his respect for Rikyu as his teacher and unease with him for being too brilliant.

One time Rikyu invited Hideyoshi to view his morning glories early one spring morning. Rikyu's garden was famous throughout the capital for its profusion and beauty. His flowers were said to grow in such abundance that they reflected the sun. Hideyoshi had not been to Rikyu's teahouse in some time and could not help but be a bit excited about seeing the famous garden.

Even in all his years as a warrior, as drenched in blood as they were, Hideyoshi had always loved flowers. Sometimes, before a great battle, as he stood at the edge of a great field of flowers, soon to become crushed by thousands of bodies of men and horses and turned into a charnel ground, he had reflected on the transience and changeableness of life as symbolized by these flowers that stood so beautifully and tenderly under the sun.

So it was with joy and pleasurable anticipation that Hideyoshi traveled to Rikyu's home that morning. But imagine his surprise when, after passing through the outer gate of the garden, he discovered that Rikyu had cut each and every flower in the garden. There was nothing there but hundreds of severed stems. Hideyoshi looked around, trying to conceal his great disappointment. He could not imagine what had come over Rikyu, but he kept his samurai composure and greeted the old tea master with as much humbleness as he could muster.

Then, after passing through the low entrance to the teahouse, Hideyoshi looked at the alcove to find just one morning glory, sitting in a simple bamboo vase. Ah, he thought, the old fox has outdone me once again! Then he settled back and allowed his mind to relax and become one with the flower.

6

The Slippery Art
of Wu Wei

Or, the Art of Doing Nothing

> The sage goes about doing nothing therefore
> is left undone.

Wu wei is one of the most difficult concepts in Daoist philosophy. Roughly translated, it means "doing nothing." Westerners who are first introduced to Daoism sometimes think the term wu wei means sitting around and doing nothing—a passive acceptance of life and a sort of mushy, hopeless attitude. Nothing could be further from the truth. Alan Watts calls wu wei

> a form of intelligence—that is, of knowing the principles, structures, and trends of human and natural affairs so well that one uses the least amount of energy in dealing with them or "the innate wisdom of the nervous system."[1]

Far from being a passive acceptance or resignation to things, it is instead an active engagement with things as they are. It is a way of working with the dynamics of any situation in order to find the path of least resistance and then following through.

The true meaning of the phrase wu wei is something like "not doing anything that is not natural" or "not doing anything that does not have its roots in Dao."

It can also mean not *over*doing anything. Laozi tells us:

> Overfilling a vessel is not as good as stopping before it is filled.
> Oversharpen a blade and it will lose its edge.
> Pile up gold and jade
> And it will be impossible to guard it.
> In going after rank and titles
> In an arrogant and haughty way
> And you will bring about your own downfall.
> Withdraw when the work is done.
> This is the way of Dao.

(Chapter 9)

It is often in overdoing something, even if it is the right thing, that we are led astray. To attain anything, even spiritual growth, in an arrogant and haughty way, is to invite our own downfall. But to do our good works and then retire, not calling attention to ourselves, is truly the way of the sage. Perhaps that is what Master Jesus meant when he talked about keeping your light under a bushel. This is something that is commented on over and over in Daoism. People who call attention to themselves, being proud of their accomplishments, be they material or spiritual, are only setting themselves up for a fall. It is better, say the sages, that one does one's deeds or spiritual practice in a quiet and humble manner and then moves on.

Wu wei is the opposite of *yu wei* or action with useless effort. It is coupled with spontaneity and a deep awareness of what is happening in any situation, allowing one to discern whether it would be better to act or not to act (which, of course, is what Hamlet was *really* talking about). It is a kind of spontaneity which, as Clae Waltham says, cannot be captured, only fostered.[2] It is a kind of perception of the currents of any situation and our place in it. Laozi says that:

> Teaching without words,
> And working without doing,
> Are understood by very few.
>
> (Chapter 43)

And:

> Do you think you can take over the universe and improve
>   it?
> I do not believe it can be done.
> The universe is sacred.
> You cannot improve it.
> If you try to change it, you will ruin it.
> If you try to grasp it, you will lose it.
>
> (Chapter 29)

Trying to hold tight to any situation, trying to figure out just what exactly is going on and, most of all, trying to control the situation through force of will or use of "knowledge" or intellectual gymnastics is foolish and will, in all probability, land us on our faces in the mud. Zhuangzi says:

> The knowledge of the ancients was perfect. How perfect? At first, they did not know that there were things. This is the most perfect knowledge; nothing can be added. Next, they knew there were things, but did not yet make distinctions between them. Next, they made distinction between them, but they did not yet

pass judgements upon them. When judgements
were passed, Dao was destroyed.[3]

Daoists are lovers of simplicity and naturalness. Zhuangzi says
the wisdom of the ancients was perfect because they did not
know there were things—they did not differentiate, they did
not catalogue, they did not separate one thing from another, one
state of mind from another, one state of being from another. In
this way they were able to remain pure and close to the original
undifferentiated Dao.

My *taiji* teacher, David Cheng, was fond of telling us it is our
mind that gets us into trouble. It is our mind, our discriminating
intellect, that creates all sorts of problems for us, then thinks it
can figure a way out of them. But then again, David said, without
our mind we would not know how to drive a car or take a bus
or make our way to taiji class! We would not understand what
language he was speaking or how to follow his movements. Our
mind is a tool, he says—a wonderful, useful tool. Sometimes, for
example, we need to discriminate; we need to be able to look
at a situation dispassionately and intelligently and see if it is a
situation or a relationship or a job or a person that is good for
us or bad for us. This is a good way to use that marvelous tool,
the mind. But let us put it back in the toolbox when we are done
with it, he would say. Let us not leave it lying around where we
can step on it or trip over it all the time.

How are we to learn to work with this slippery concept, wu
wei? The old maxim "learn by doing" applies here as well as
anywhere else. It is a matter of going slowly, the slower the better.
The wonderful dance of taiji is a perfect example of wu wei in
action. The gentle movements are done as slowly as possible, so
that it becomes a sort of dancing meditation.

Often we find ourselves in trouble simply because we are
going too fast, disregarding signs of trouble that we would have
seen if only we had been going a little slower. All too often we
get caught up in the rush; our whole culture is based on it. Get

ahead! Do it now! So stop to listen quietly to the voices within—the still, small voices as well as the loud and clear ones. It is hard, if not downright impossible, to hear them when we are going fast, listening instead to the constant blare of the world around us. *Sometimes the right thing to do is not to do anything.*

Wu wei is an attitude, an approach to life itself. When we become sensitive to the current of change all around us we will be able to make intelligent decisions at all times, using the innate wisdom of our bodies and energy systems as well as our minds. As A.C. Graham, in his excellent translation of *The Book of Lieh Tzu*, says, "Nowhere is there a principle which is right in all circumstances, or an action that is wrong in all circumstances."[4]

Wu wei is learning how to conserve our energy and not spend it frivolously or in fear or confusion. Sometimes it is far easier and actually in our best interest and in the best interest of the actual situation to do nothing or to find some way around the situation rather than trying to go through it.

We may be sick or injured and lying in bed, trying hard to figure out what is going on, why this is happening to us and when it will be over. While the body, mind and spirit are tied up in knots trying to decipher this maddening puzzle, we are getting nowhere, slowly. How much easier, though it takes a little practice, to just let go and let be what is and learn how to be okay while we are not feeling okay. Sometimes there just is not anything to do, and the best course is to relax and and do nothing. Later on the situation may change and there will be something that we *can* do to help ourselves. Then, with the same grace that we did nothing, we can do something.

Oftentimes doing something is not better, more important or even more helpful than doing nothing. When we feel stuck and unable to move, what we are actually doing is storing energy to be able to make a move, or the kind of move that will actually mean something. Like water, our energy must slowly collect before it can spill over the dam. Often when we think we shall never get out of a rut or never be able to move again, being patient and conserving our energy will help us make an even greater move when the time is right.

By learning to relax and discover the intrinsic flow of events that contain and are contained by our lives we can reach some measure of security and perhaps even wisdom. Zhuangzi likens this state to that of a drunken man:

> A drunken man falls out of a cart; though he may suffer, he does not die. His bones are the same as other people's; but he meets the accident in a different way. His spirit is the condition of security. He is not conscious of riding in the cart; neither is he conscious of falling out of it. Ideas of life, death and fear cannot penetrate his breast; and so he does not suffer from contact with objective circumstances. And if such security is to be got from wine, how much more is to be gotten from spontaneity?[5]

In this passage, Zhuangzi describes wu wei as spontaneity, a total indentification with the present moment. For in reality there is no other moment than the one we are in. So then, how to develop this sense of spontaneity, this sensitivity to the here and now? A.C. Graham says:

> If he wishes to return to the Way he must discard knowledge, cease to make distinctions, refuse to impose his will and his principles on nature, recover the spontaneity of the newborn child, allow his actions to be "so of themselves" *like physical processes* [author's italics].[6]

It is in applying the principles of wu wei to our life that we truly begin to understand and experience Tea Mind or Cha Dao. By not forcing, by going with the flow, by letting things develop in their own time, by not being attached to outcomes, by giving ourselves time to "just be"—through meditation, walking in nature, through whatever activity or non-activity that allows us to feel the spaciousness of our true self, by being comfortable with not being okay sometimes—these are all ways to open ourselves to the ongoing, ever-flowing stream of life both within and around us.

In the Wu Wei Way of Tea we are able to find ourselves again, we are able to reconnect and realign ourselves with the great Way or Dao. And in that connection we can begin to heal, to find the path to wholeness. And in this Way we can open ourselves to new experiences, new ways of seeing and being, new attitudes and ways of looking at the world and our place in it.

Notes

1. Ibid., p.76.
2. Clae Waltham (1971) *Chuang Tzu: Genius of the Absurd*, p.19.
3. Fung Yu-Lan (1973) *A History of Chinese Philosophy: Volume I*, p.239.
4. Graham, *The Book of Lieh Tzu*, p.163.
5. Herbert, A. Giles (1926) *Chuang-Tzu: Mystic, Moralist, and Social Reformer*, p.19.
6. Graham, *The Book of Lieh Tzu*, p.3.

7

One Last Cup

Sen Rikyu sat alone after bidding farewell to the guests who had come for his last tea ceremony. In these last few precious moments he had left on this earth, he reflected on his long life, both as a tea master and Zen practitioner, and on his often-rocky relationship with the Taiko, Hideyoshi. It was true that the often-tempestuous ruler had granted him many favors and they had spent many wonderful hours in Rikyu's simple and small tea hut. Hideyoshi had his famous gold teahouse which he took with him when he visited the capital but Rikyu knew that the ruler of all Japan felt most at home in Rikyu's simple and austere teahouse.

As he sat there in the early morning light, listening to the sounds of the birds in the trees above him and the rustle of the leaves surrounding him, Rikyu knew in his heart that he had finally gone too far and had angered the Taiko beyond measure. He supposed that he had tried to live too far above his station and this is what it had come to.

Rikyu remembered those early days when he had become the teacher, friend and confidant of the Taiko. It was true that

Hideyoshi was uncouth and rough in many ways, due to his difficult life as a poor son of simple farmers and as a warrior, yet sometimes when Rikyu was serving him tea in his simple, unostentatious manner, he could see the Taiko relax and visibly enter the timeless time of tea, that time when he could forget all his problems and be enveloped in the slow, depthless moments of the Way of Tea.

This Way of Tea, which Rikyu had served all his long life, he remembered long ago when he had written his famous poem on tea.

> The Way of Tea is nothing but this:
> First you boil the water,
> And then you make the tea
> And then you drink it.

Yes, it was true that he had lived for that moment for so many years. But then it seemed that he had become corrupt with becoming the chosen one of the Taiko. He had lost his way and had begun to amass riches and fame which were now dragging him down to his death.

He and Hideyoshi had clashed many times. It was, after all, impossible to avoid completely. Hideyoshi was volatile and moody. He had suffered much in his life and had never completely gotten over the wounds that he had received, both on the battlefield and in his wild and impoverished youth. But he had succeeded where no one else had in uniting all of Japan. Yet it had come at a terrible cost, both in bloodshed and in the deaths of many, many warriors and peasants. Rikyu knew that Hideyoshi suffered from bad dreams, dreams in which he relived his early days, back when he had been called Monkey because of his rough features. He had been mocked and made fun of but had borne it well when he could and had fought when he could not. Now he was ruler of a great land but he could still remember the torments of his youth. His desire to become a cultured leader, both feared and respected by his people, had forced him to work extremely hard on his own cultivation. The Way of Tea was one avenue of his diligent self-cultivation.

He remembered the time he had cut all of his precious morning glories, which had been famous all over the capital, just to teach Hideyoshi a lesson about attachment. He could see that the Taiko was very upset when he entered the tea hut and saw the one lone flower in the place of honor in the tokonoma but he had held his temper and even seemed to relax after a while and enjoy the tea ceremony. They had never spoken of it afterwards but Rikyu had hoped that something of his message had gotten through. Rikyu remembered with a wince how painful it had been for him to cut all his lovely flowers and how he had felt that the lesson he had been imparting to Hideyoshi had also been for himself.

But Rikyu knew that he had presumed greatly on his friendship with the Taiko. He knew that his refusal to have his daughter become a concubine of the Taiko had angered Hideyoshi greatly. But Rikyu loved his daughter greatly and the thought of her being shut up in the great house of the Lord, there to wither away while Hideyoshi spent all his time traveling about the country, had forced him to say no to the ruler of all Japan. Hideyoshi's face had darkened and he had strode out of Rikyu's house like the fierce and uncouth warrior he was, though he said nothing, not wishing to lower himself to arguing with one of his subjects. He could, of course, have simply taken the girl, but Rikyu was famous and he did not wish to lose his dignity in the eyes of the people.

And so they had quarreled and Hideyoshi now came very seldom to his teacher's small tea hut. Then, recently, Rikyu had gone too far. He had ordered a great statue of himself to be erected at the temple at Kaitoku-ji, which he had supported generously over the years, in memory of his early days there. But when Hideyoshi visited there and saw the great statue of Rikyu, he had become extremely angry and, for the first time, he listened to the malicious lies that others told about the tea master—of how he had planned on poisoning the ruler with a cup of tea—and had ordered Rikyu to commit *seppuku*, ritual suicide.

Of course Rikyu could have apologized; he could have called upon their long friendship, but in his heart he knew that he had lost the Way and his way in it. He realized that the time had come to shed his earthly form. And so he had put all his affairs in order and called upon an old friend of the samurai class to be his attendant and take off his head after he had made the cuts to his abdomen that the ritual called for. Dressed all in white, Rikyu would, after composing himself in meditation, open his kimono and, taking his knife, would plunge it into his abdomen and cut from left to right and then slightly upward. It was then that his attendant would swing his sword in a graceful arc and take off Rikyu's head, leaving one small bit of flesh so that the head would not roll in an unsightly fashion.

Now, having served tea one last time, having drunk one last cup of tea and then deliberately broken the bowl he had drunk from, and having given away all his simple yet priceless tea utensils, he sat and composed his death poem.

> I raise my sword,
> So long in my possession,
> The time has come
> To throw it up to the heavens!

When he had been drinking that one last cup of tea, he had remembered the old Zen story of the man who, having fallen off a cliff, had hung on for dear life from a root, with sharp rocks waiting below and a tiger prowling above, and had discovered a tiny strawberry plant growing out of the side of the cliff with one berry on it. There suspended between life and death he reached out one shaky arm to pick it and brought it to his mouth and thought to himself, how sweet the taste!

Rikyu had lived a long and interesting life and now he sat, suspended between life and death, still tasting the bitter and sweet taste of the last cup of tea in his mouth. He hoped that his friend would be swift with his sword and not wait until he had made all the cuts. He hoped that his family would be safe from the anger of the Taiko. He hoped that his small contribution to the Way of Tea would live on after him. He hoped that his small soul would fly away at his death and join the Great Soul that encompassed all of life.

He sat very still, breathing deeply and slowly. He heard the footsteps of his attendant coming down the hall. He felt the cares of the world lift away from him, just as his spirit would at death. He gave silent thanks for all that he had learned and experienced in the Way of Tea, the Way of Life. He bowed slightly in the direction of the sunrise and closed his eyes. He sat and waited for the door to slide open and for the heavy footsteps of the samurai to enter the room and he once again savored the sublime taste of that one last cup of tea.

8

The Uncarved Block

The principles treasured by the Daoist are simplicity, equilibrium, harmony and quietude[1]

The principle of the Uncarved Block or *P'u* in Chinese is an essential element of Daoist philosophy and practice. It is the concept of the simple, uncluttered and natural man and woman and their way of life. This way of being in the world is in perfect accord, of course, with the teachings of Laozi and Zhuangzi.

Laozi says:

Fame or self: Which matters more?
Self or wealth: Which is more precious?
Gain or loss: Which is more painful?

He who is attached to things will suffer much.
He who saves will suffer heavy loss.
He who knows when to stop does not find himself in
   trouble.
He will stay forever safe.

(Chapter 44)

The ancient Daoists not only were content to live simple, natural lives but actually felt there was a solid advantage to doing so. It is not necessary to drop out and live in the mountains away from the world in order to live a simple, natural life. What we are actually talking about is an *internal* state of simplicity and naturalness. We may be involved in all kinds of things, from running a large clinic to teaching a group of children or overseeing a complicated business. Yet all of this need not stop us from having internal simplicity and naturalness.

It is when we allow outside pressures and complications to take up residence within us that we run into trouble and lose our sense of safety and spontaneity, which to Daoists is very serious indeed. How often do we meet someone at a party or other gathering and are asked by way of introduction, "So what is it that you do?," as if a description of our work life defines us? Why are we not asked or why do we not ask, "What is it that interests you in life? What turns you on?" That information would probably go much further in describing or defining us to others and to ourselves.

Remember the principle of wu wei? It is often in *not doing* that we get the most done! Often *not doing* defines who we are much more thoroughly than all the *doing* we could possible produce. Yet we get caught up in an urge to produce to some extent. After all, if I were following the principle of wu wei exactly, I would not even be writing this book!

It is said that the Dao will manifest itself to everyone, sooner or later. There is no rush or even set time when this will or should happen. But all the teachers, both ancient and modern, stress that it is in the natural simplicity of our being that we can best manifest and embrace the Dao. The question is, how do we do this?

Hua-Ching Ni says: "A natural human being is directed by his spiritual energy and causes appropriate responses not by his need, but by his pure spontaneity."[2]

Remember, spontaneity is something that rises from deep within our true nature and cannot be artificially produced. This spontaneity also has something of the "holy fool" in it.

Indeed, there is a vast tradition of "holy fools" throughout the world. Here, however, we will limit ourselves to the Daoist version of this interesting and amusing figure.

N.J. Girardot describes him thus:

> Taoist images of madness are related to the mystical experience of the chaos condition and to the unique effortless freedom of wu wei, the sage's playful freedom beyond human, or even humane, bounds. The Taoist as a "demented drifter" is aloof and indifferent to the normal order of the world. From the perspective of his belly knowledge, the Taoist is a wayfarer who knows that "the way things appear to be— permanent, predictable, manageable—is not the way things really are in an ultimate vision of the real."[3]

The "holy fool" is one who is not actually a fool in the real sense, but is called that by a society that does not understand his or her actions. This is because the Daoist is operating outside of the norm, or what society at large considers normal. To the highly rigid and structured Confucian society of the Han dynasty and beyond, the Daoists, with their free and "wild" (in the sense of natural) ways, were often regarded as fools and rebellious outcasts, content to live "in the world but not of it."

And, because they were basing their understanding and approach to life on something other than the status quo, they were considered rebels and malcontents or just empty-headed dreamers. It was a state not always comfortable for them either.

As Laozi puts it so poignantly:

> Other people have more than enough,
> But I alone seem to have lost everything.
> I am foolish!
> Other people are clear
> While I alone am confused.
> Other people are clever
> While I am dull.
> I feel lost at sea,
> Tossed about on the winds of a storm.
> Everyone else has things to do
> While I appear dull and stupid.
> I am different from the others,
> Because I am nourished by the Great Mother.

(Chapter 20)

This is a beautiful way to describe the often sad feeling of being different or cut off from the crowd. Daoists have to get used to going their own way and being misunderstood, or even ridiculed because of their beliefs and way of life. But is it not better to be called a fool than to actually be one? After all, is not the unhealthy, unbalanced and unconscious way that most people live true foolishness?

When we first become aware and sensitive to the subtle currents of energy in our being—spiritual, physical and emotional—it can be painful. Many of us are not used to being particularly sensitive and we sometimes come up hard against our limitations, created both by the world and by ourselves. We may feel alienated and cut off from those around us who are busy rushing after the next thrill, the next high, the next desperate way of trying to be real.

While there are, even today, many students and followers of the Way, they are often hard to identify. You may see a wide-eyed, open-ended look that is offered when you least expect it, or perhaps a certain loose-limbed way of walking, a sign of one who is attuned to his or her own energy flow. You may encounter an attitude toward healing or an openness to the use of herbs or acupuncture, or a way of unaffected talking, and a deep awareness of the importance of good listening. Or else you may hear a good strong laugh, coming from deep in the belly, a laugh that says yes, I am a believer in the sanctity and miraculous unfolding of each precious moment in the Dao and I am willing to share that feeling, that awareness, that experience with you.

There is also the shared knowledge that most of what passes for "reality" in the collective unconscious is actually a huge joke, a play, a pantomime.

To the Daoists, what we experience on the material plane is as real as the nose on our face. Yet at the same time it is also a bit of a dream. Zhuangzi once dreamed that he was a butterfly, flitting merrily about the multicolored flowers. When he awoke he exclaimed, "How is it that I can be sure that instead of Zhuangzi dreaming that I am a butterfly, I am not a butterfly dreaming that I am Zhuangzi?"

In another place he says:

> People in general bustle about here and there. The sage seems stupid and without "knowledge." When people dream they do not know that they are dreaming. In their dream state they may even pretend to interpret dreams. Only when they truly awaken do they begin to know that they have been dreaming. By and by will come the Great Awakening, and then we shall find out that life itself is a great dream. All the while fools think that they are awake, and that they have knowledge. They go on making distinctions, they differentiate between princes and grooms. How stupid!

The experience of "life as a dream" frees us from the awful burden of always having to do it right, of toiling under the enormous weight of having to be on the job at all times. It frees us also to make mistakes and allows us the freedom, the privilege, of starting over again, time after time if need be. And, most of all, it frees us to change, to begin anew, to metamorphosize into whatever lovely and colorful butterfly we always wanted to be but never felt the permission or strength to become.

Remember, the Dao does not judge, it does not punish, it does not condemn. We do that ourselves. And as we judge, so also can we forgive ourselves and others who have wronged us through their own mistaken sense of reality. And we find, in that forgiveness, an even greater sense of freedom and unlimited potential—for growth, exploration, and an enlarged sense of the Dao and our place in it.

Through forgiveness, through trust, through taking chances with ourselves and others, and through returning to our "original nature"—our own sweet simple and natural self, our own "uncarved block"—we can begin the journey that leads back to its beginning, to our original nature, or Dao.

Once, after a particularly poignant lesson by his teacher, Lieh Tzu decided that, in truth, he had never learned anything, so he went home and for three years did not leave his house.

> He cooked meals for his wife,
> Served food to his pigs as though they were human,
> Treated all things as equally as his kin,
> From carved jade he returned to the unhewn block,
> Till his single shape stood forth, detached from all things.
> He was free of tangles
> Once and for all, to the end of his life.[4]

Notes

1.   Hua-Ching Ni (1979b) *The Taoist Inner View of the Universe and the Immortal Realm*, p.38
2.   Hua-Ching Ni (1979a) *Tao: The Subtle Universal Law and the Integral Way of Life*, p.110.
3.   N.J. Girardot (1983) *Myth and Meaning in Early Daoism*.
4.   A.C. Graham (1960) *The Book of Lieh Tzu*, p.49.

9

The Man Who Knew Too Much

A Tale of Tea and Enlightenment

There was once a great master who had studied all the esoteric knowledge and all the spiritual teachings of all the great masters. He had traveled for many years all around the world, studying with this master and that. He had read all the great books that had been written and had spent years in deep meditation high in the mountains of the Himalayas. He had practiced secret tantric rites, both with a female consort and with the bones of ancient masters. He had reflected on himself as a numinous being as well as a bony skull, waiting for death for release from the material world. He himself had written many dense and obtuse works of spiritual knowledge. He had taught at many of the great universities as well as the great spiritual centers around the world. He had many students, many of whom would have worshiped him if he had allowed it.

He had had many lovers and had fathered numerous children, all of whom, he had announced, would grow up to be sages. He had looked death in the face and laughed, he had spent vast sums of money, most of it donated to him by his many wealthy students, building grand temples and ashrams, but he never stayed at one of them for long, for he was a restless spirit and was always drawn on to the next new teacher, the next new lover, the next new spiritual experience.

He could control his body temperature and had studied *tumo* with Tibetan monks and could dry a dozen wet sheets they had wrapped around him as he sat by a freezing lake high in the Himalayas. He had meditated with Shiva-worshiping sadhus in India and had smoked vast quantities of hashish with them as they sat meditating by the burning ghats along the sacred Ganges. He had watched many people's bodies transform from human beings to piles of glowing ash.

He was famous and rich and very, very successful; many called him enlightened, but he was not satisfied. He was restless but could not say what it was he was restless about. He felt he was missing out on something very important and perhaps even crucial but he could not say what that very important and crucial thing was. All he knew was that he did not have it and he felt he would never be whole until he did.

He stopped traveling, stopped public speaking and writing, and shut himself deep within his meditation chamber. He refused food and drank only a small amount of fruit juice a day, just enough to keep himself alive while he went deep inside himself to find what it was that he was missing.

But after many days of this he felt no closer to the elusive something than when he had started, and he became very angry. Then he became very depressed. He sat listlessly in his room, deep in the heart of his ashram, and looked idly out the window and sighed deep, sad sighs.

Then one day one of his students begged for an audience with him, saying that he had made a great discovery and wanted to share it with his guru. So the great master decided that he was so completely bored that he would speak with someone, even if it was a student, and a not very advanced one either.

So imagine when this student came into his presence, and, after making obeisance to him, told him that he had found a great teacher, one who far surpassed all other teachers, one who was as the sun to the moon, as a shining lotus flower to a weed, whose immense knowledge dwarfed all other spiritual teachers.

The master began, in spite of himself, to become interested. He was sure that he had already met all the great masters of the age and had gleaned from them whatever knowledge they possessed. But perhaps there was still yet one whom he had not met and who might have an answer to his problem. In spite of himself, he was becoming interested. His student then told him where this great teacher could be found. It was in a little teashop which was located in a run-down part of the city, upstairs from a laundry. This does not sound promising, said the great master to himself, but he decided he would go there anyway and see if there was not some crumb of knowledge he could glean from this new teacher.

So, after consulting his star chart and other divinatory tools for an auspicious day, he followed his student's directions and traveled to a part of the city where he had never been before. As he picked his way through the congested streets he found himself becoming more and more convinced that he was wasting his time. There can't be any sort of realized master in this part of town, he thought to himself. He knew that great masters always dwelt in the mountains where they could breathe the pure air and be closer to the spiritual realm, or else deep within sacred caves where they could not be polluted by the dust of the world, or else in ashrams or temples, where they could be closer to the divine energy of the gods.

And so, as he picked his way through the mounds of trash and dog feces (he was, as usual, wearing sandals, which had cost a lot of money and which he did not want to be smeared with dog feces), he began to have greater and greater doubts. But he decided to go on and see it through to the end. After all, if he could spend all that time in the Himalayas studying arcane tantric arts and smoke all that pungent and incredibly potent hashish with the sadhus while they watched the fat bubble on the bodies of the dead, he figured he could handle traveling through these nasty streets.

After some time he came to the laundry, from which clouds of odoriferous steam emerged, and, after poking around for some time, found a set of dilapidated steps leading up to the second floor. He climbed up the stairs, which squeaked and squawked under his feet and threatened to crumble before his weight with every step until he found himself at the door to the teashop. Not that there was any written sign there indicating there was a business there but there was a crude picture of a teapot with steam rising out of its spout in the shape of a dragon so he figured he was in the right place.

He tried knocking a few times but when that got no response he tried the door and, finding it unlocked, he opened it and entered the tiny and cluttered shop. No one was about and he spent a few minutes surveying the room. It was indeed very small and was filled with shelf after shelf of various clay jars of tea. There were also many clay teapots, some of them fantastically shaped and most of them covered in a thin film of dust.

He looked around some more until he found a small table with several tiny stools in front of it, the very low stools like the ones used by the peasants in China. He wondered where the proprietor could be and was on the point of leaving when suddenly a door he had not noticed before opened at the back of the room, and a very old and very odd-looking man came through. He was so bent over that his head was aligned with his waist and he needed to look up and twist his neck around so that he could see his visitor.

"Ah," he said, with a great smile, which seemed to emerge from out of his wrinkled face like the sun coming out of a cloud. "I did not know I had a customer. Please forgive my inattentiveness. I'm afraid I have no excuse." And he tried to bow a little lower but he was already so hunched over that to bow any further was impossible.

The master was feeling a bit uncomfortable and would have liked to have left but the little man was smiling so sweetly at him that he decided it would have been very rude and so he decided to take a few moments to be cordial to this funny-looking old man and then be on his way.

The old man pointed to one of the tiny stools and invited the master to sit. The stool looked so small and old and fragile that the master was very sure it would not support his weight but, in the interest of politeness, he decided to try it. As he lowered himself onto the stool he was surprised to find it held up very well. He relaxed then and breathed out a deep sigh. For some strange reason this miniature stool felt more comfortable than the throne he usually sat upon when receiving pilgrims at the ashram.

The old man smiled again at him and said, in a very loud voice, "Please wait a moment, good sire, while I make us some tea."

The master began to protest that this was not needed but cut himself off. Perhaps it *would* be nice to have a hot cup of tea before he left, he thought to himself. So he sat and watched as the old man shuffled around the room in a sort of odd fashion that almost looked as though he were floating a little above the floor.

"I have some very good *Lung Jing*, Dragon Well, tea here from a friend who lives in Hangzhou," he said, in that loud voice. "I just can't exactly remember what I did with it," he added, while searching through the many jars that sat upon the shelves. "Ah," he said at last, "here it is." He shuffled on over to the table where the master sat and plopped himself down on the stool opposite him. "Now we shall drink some tea and become acquainted." Here he looked over expectantly at the master, who looked back at him, feeling more curious by the moment about just who this old man was.

Suddenly the old man started. "Oh dear," he said, "I forgot to get the water!" And here he jumped up and shuffled across the room again in his funny floating way and disappeared behind the door from which he had emerged earlier. In just a moment he was back again, carrying a steaming kettle of hot water. "I had just put it on right before you arrived," he said. "I have been so looking forward to this meeting."

The master wondered to himself how in the world the old man had known of his visit before he had arrived but decided that his student had probably told him. For some reason he felt very relaxed there, sitting on the ridiculously small stool looking over as the old man placed a small handful of tea leaves into a small clay teapot. This Dragon Well tea, the master knew, was a favorite of poets and artists. He watched as the old man then poured the water onto the leaves and then put the lid onto the pot.

"We must wait for a moment or two while the water and the leaves dance together," said the old man, looking over at the master with such a sweet and accepting gaze that he felt a little flushed. He was used to people looking at him in awe and even worshipfully but this was different. The old man looked over at him in complete acceptance he felt, not because of who he was or what his attainments were, but just as a fellow traveler on the road of life. Yet it was more than that. It was as if the old man could see right down deep into his heart and, upon seeing the real essence of his being, not only accepted him but even approved of him. Again, he had the feeling that to the old man he was not the great master that most people saw but just a fellow human being and worthy to be accepted and treated with warmth and friendship.

The master felt something stir within him as he sat there. Perhaps this old man truly was a great teacher. Perhaps he had the answer to the question that had plagued him these last few years.

He wanted to speak up right then and there but, for some reason, felt shy about doing so. This is odd, he thought to himself, he had never felt this sense of shyness with anyone before, not even the Dalai Lama or any of the other great teachers and masters he had met. He decided to hold his tongue for the moment and see what the old man said.

The old man suddenly reached over to the teapot and began pouring the steaming liquid into round clay cups. "I find that when I get anxious or stressed, all it takes is a good cup of tea to make things right again. That is," and here he looked over at the master with a quick and penetrating gaze, "if I truly relax and allow the tea to do its work on my soul."

Now that is an odd thing to say about a cup of tea, thought the master to himself. He reached over and picked up his cup and made to drink it. "Wait," said the old man. "We must first inhale the rich aroma of the tea and let it make its way down into our bodies and souls."

There was that strange phrase again, thought the master, as if tea could have an effect on our souls. But he dutifully took up his cup and held it before his nose and inhaled deeply. Yes, he thought, this is good tea. The aroma seemed to enter his nose and reach down into his heart. He felt something unclench there. He wondered what it was.

"Now we drink," said the old man and lifted the cup to his lips and drank. The master did the same. It was strange but, as the tea entered his mouth, he felt his whole being stretch forward to receive it. I wonder if the old man has bewitched this tea, he thought to himself, and felt a short pang of fear but, just as quickly, he put that thought out of his mind and just allowed the sweet goodness of the tea to enter his being. He felt himself relaxing in a way he hadn't for some time.

The old man was looking at him over the rim of his cup. While it was true he was still terribly bent over, at the same time it looked as though he was sitting straight and tall and looking over at the master on an equal level. The master shook his head and again the old man was bent over and drinking his cup of tea with both hands.

"You know," said the old man, "tea once saved my life."

At this the master looked up expectantly. He wondered how this could be so. He had always loved a good story and he looked forward to this one.

"It was during the so-called Great Proletariat Cultural Revolution," he said. "Such a dark time." Here he stopped and took another sip of this tea. His body was so bent over that he seemed to be having some trouble swallowing. But after a moment he went on. "The Red Guards had come to my home town and set about destroying the Four Olds.[1] They were children really, so young. Yet they were willful and destructive children and they were on a mission to destroy the old traditions and had the blessing of the Great Helmsman. They had already smashed everything in the local temple and had beaten the few priests that had not run off. They had made a huge bonfire of all the paintings and books that they had torn out of the villagers' homes. Some of these had been in families for generations. People were crying but the Red Guards only beat them when they tried to resist or even when they expressed their emotions about what was happening.

"I stood on the edge of the crowd. I had no belongings that interested the Red Guards. Or at least not at first. But after looking through my house the first time and not finding anything of value, they decided to look a little closer. I had, of course, hidden anything of value out back in the privy before they came."

"How did you know they were coming?" asked the master.

"Oh," said the old man, "the tea told me. Just as it did about you."

The master was not sure he had heard right. "Does the tea speak to you then?" he asked.

"Oh yes," replied the old man. "It always has." He cleared his throat and went on. "The second time they came through they found a small teapot that had been in my family for seven generations. It was such a small and ugly thing that I had not thought to hide it. But, as it was obviously old, even ancient, it was a great find for the Red Guards.

"'What is this?' they shouted, spitting in my face in their excitement. 'This looks like contraband from the Imperial Feudal times. You should have turned this in the first time we came here. But instead you sought to hide it from us,' which was ridiculous since it sat right up on a shelf in plain sight. But they were rapturous at their find. I could see that, in their excitement, they meant to use me as an example. They raged around my small house, ripping shelves down and destroying all my pitiful furniture. Meanwhile several of them guarded me, lest I escape.

"When they were done they held up the very small, old and very ugly teapot in my face and shouted, 'Why do you hide this old feudal thing from us? Why did you not destroy this as you were supposed to?' They actually spat in my face they were so excited. So I said the first thing that popped into my head. 'Because it's magic!' I shouted.

"This stopped them in their tracks. Because, you know, even if a few of them were from the city most of the Red Guards were country boys and girls. They did not have the sophistication of their fellows from the big city.

"I looked at them and saw so many emotions playing across their faces. The city ones were, of course, contemptuous, but I could see that the country ones believed, almost against their will, a little of what I had said.

"'What do you mean, magic?' they thundered and threw me violently to the floor, hurting my back. 'There is no such thing in modern China!' They kicked me then and would have done much worse but I could see that a few of them wanted to know more about what I was saying. 'Show us this magic,' they shouted, shoving the teapot into my face.

"I wasn't sure what to do. So I gingerly reached out for the teapot and got up from the floor. 'I need to heat some water,' I said, 'so you can see the magic.' When they allowed me to rise and hobble over to the stove, I knew I had them. The ones from the city were, of course, sneering at me, but the country ones, while they also tried to sneer, looked at me as if I might decide to sprout wings and fly away. Many of them had grown up around priests and shamans and some part of them still believed in the old ways, even if they were not supposed to.

"I heated water for the tea. I had some *Lung Jing* tea left, the same kind we are drinking now. I brought the water to a boil and then let it sit a moment. 'What are you doing?' shouted the Red Guards, especially the city ones. 'I am waiting for the water to transform,' I told them. This caused much muttering and I could see the city ones were going to lose their patience soon if I did not produce something good.

"After waiting a few moments I began to pour the water into the teapot, which I had filled with a huge handful of tea leaves. In reality, it only takes a small amount of high quality tea to brew good tea but I wasn't going to take any chances. After I poured the water I set the teapot on the counter and walked over to the other side of the room. 'What are you doing?' they shouted. 'I am now waiting for the marriage of the tea and water to finish. Then you will see some magic.'

"Of course this made them all very upset. The city ones were running out of patience with me and I could see the violence in their eyes. But the country ones wanted to make sure. 'Hold on,' they said to the others. 'He is just a stupid old man and when we see that he has no magic we will beat him and break his ugly old teapot.'

"This seemed to calm the city ones down a bit and they smiled in anticipation of the good beating they were going to give me. After a few more minutes I went over to the teapot, which now held a strong brew of tea. 'You have broken all my cups,' I said to them. 'We will have to drink out of the pot itself.' I knew that many country people did not use teacups but just drank straight out of the teapot so the country ones did not think that strange.

"'I will drink first,' I said and raised the teapot to my mouth. They all stood around me then, their muscles tense, as if they were getting ready to flee at a moment's notice. I took a small sip and shouted 'Long life to Chairman Mao!' Of course they all had to shout along with me. I took another small sip and shouted 'Ten Thousand Years for Chairman Mao!' Of course I knew I was taking a chance with this one. The phrase Ten Thousand Years was what they used to say to the emperor. But I was counting on the fact that, even though Mao was not, in name, the emperor, to these youngsters he might as well have called himself that, so exalted was he to them.

"So I decided to go out on a limb. 'I now call upon all the spirits of this village to enter this teapot in the name of the great Chairman Mao!' I held the teapot over my head and shook it a bit, as if unseen beings were entering it. Then I lowered it and offered it to the Red Guards. 'Please drink to Chairman Mao,' I said to them. One by one they came forward to drink from the pot. Of course, once I had dedicated it to their great leader they would not dare to turn me down. One by one they came forward and drank from the teapot.

"What they were not prepared for was the electric tingle of the tea as it entered their mouths. I could see each one of them jump as they tasted it. I could see that the country ones were sure that spirits had entered it. Even some of the city ones, I could see, were convinced that *something* had altered the tea. Of course what they did not know, and would never know if I could help it, was that, in addition to the great amount of tea I had filled the teapot with, I had also surreptitiously dumped a good amount of red pepper powder into it. The strong spice had been left on the counter from the night before when I had used it to make my favorite Szechwan dish, Kung Po Dofu.

"Once the teapot was emptied they acted very differently than before. They offered the teapot back to me, almost shyly. A few of them even bowed to me. The city ones were still a little unconvinced and said to me, 'Remember next time, old man, not to try and trick us. We will not be so lenient with you then!'

"I smiled and bowed to them, holding the teapot to my chest. The pain in my back from when they had thrown me to the floor was already beginning to travel up my spine but I held back my tears and smiled at them. 'Love live Chairman Mao,' I called to them, brandishing the teapot.

"After they finally left I collapsed to the floor, the pain in my back so strong I wept aloud with it. Later on one of my neighbors came by to check up on me and found me there on the floor and helped me to my bed. I was babbling by this time. It was the pepper I kept saying, it was just the pepper. 'What are you talking about?' asked my neighbor. I tried to tell her about tricking the Red Guards but I'm afraid I made very little sense. Finally I blurted out, 'In the teapot, look and see.' So she went over to the counter where I had laid the teapot before I collapsed to the floor. She opened the top and smelled it. She looked at me curiously. Finally she upended the pot and shook out the last few drops of tea there. 'This tea tastes fine,' she said. 'It is a little strong but it is good Dragon Well.'

"'Bring it here,' I said and she dutifully brought it over to me. I opened the lid myself and smelled. It smelled like tea and nothing else. I cautiously dipped my finger into the mass of damp tea leaves and brought it to my lips. Nothing but the taste of tea. But what had happened to the pepper that I was sure I had put into it?

"'On the contrary,' I said, 'red pepper.' My neighbor went to the counter and looked around. 'Things are a bit of a mess here,' she said, shaking her head. 'But there is no red pepper, only the dust from the bottom of the tea canister.'

"I asked myself how this could be true. I was sure I had put red pepper in the teapot, not tea dust. I wondered what had made the tea so hot and spicy. Could it really have been the local spirits entering it? Whatever it was, I thought, it had saved my life. Yes, I was in pain and the injury did leave me as you see me now but if

I had been wrong and the tea had not worked its miracle on the ferocious Red Guards, they would have surely killed me."

The tea in their cups was gone now and the old man filled the teapot with hot water once again. The master sat there wondering what to say. He had heard more amazing stories than this one on his travels around the world but, for some reason, he felt very touched by this one. Maybe it was the sweet smile of the old man who, having suffered so much, seemed to be happy and content here in his tiny shop.

Perhaps, he thought to himself, he is the teacher that I have been searching for. He decided to tell the old man who he was and what his accomplishments were. He would list for him the various initiations he had gone through, what spiritual powers he had attained, what masters he had already studied under these long years, how many people he had already touched with his spiritual force, how many people he had healed, how famous he was. He knew, of course, that he was bragging but it seemed important to him to establish himself in the old man's eyes before the old man might impart something of his vast wisdom to him.

He began to speak, but just as he did the old man got up from the table and came over to the master's side of the table. "Allow me to fill your cup," he said, warmly. He tipped the pot of hot tea into the master's cup. On and on he went until it began to spill over and run all over the table. Surely he sees what he is doing, thought the master. He was about to say something as the old man continued to pour hot tea until it ran over the edge of the table onto his lap!

He leapt up, his thighs having been scalded with the hot tea and sputtered, "Do you not see what you are doing, old man? You have poured hot tea all over my lap!"

The old man then stopped pouring the tea and looked up at the master with a gentle smile. "I know very well what I have done," he said. "Your mind and heart are so full of your past accomplishments my friend that I am afraid, just as with this cup, there is no room for me to fit anything else into it."

The master wobbled a little and sank suddenly back down onto the tiny stool. He felt something move within him and he was flooded with tears. It was true, he was already filled to the brim. How could anyone reach him the way he was? He remembered something he had read long ago from the *Daodejing*, the sacred book of the Daoists.

> In the world of knowledge,
> Every day something is added.
> In the world of Dao,
> Every day something is let go.

He lowered his head and bowed to the old man. He bowed so low that his head was actually lower than that of the bent old man. "Teacher," he exclaimed. "You are right. Please enlighten me!"

The old man continued to sit there and smile at the master. The master felt vast moving in his being and he began to weep. And as he did so he felt all the accumulation of his spiritual quest pour out of him along with his tears. He sat and wept for a long time, so great were his accumulations. When at last he felt empty he lifted his head to the old man.

"Please," he said, as he held out his teacup. "May I have some more tea?"

It is said that this man who knew too much spent much of his time visiting the old tea master and drinking many kinds of tea with him. They spoke of this and that and the old man never seemed to be sharing anything special, but when the master returned home after drinking tea with the tea master he always felt refreshed and full of joy.

Note

1. The Four Olds are old customs, old ideas, old culture and old habits.

10

The Value of Worthlessness

Thirty spoke gather around one hub.
It is this empty space
That creates the cart wheel.
Clay is shaped to form a vessel.
It is the empty space inside
Which makes it useful.
When cutting out space for doors and windows
It is the empy spaces which makes them useful.
Therefore, having things leads to profit.
While not having leads to usefulness.

(Chapter 11)

Once a man came to see Zhuangzi and complained about a tree he owned. "It is huge," he says. "It covers my whole yard. It is very old and has been there for as long as anyone in the village can remember. Yet it is an ugly old thing. Its branches are so twisted and knotted that they are perfectly useless for timber. The wood is so hard it resists all axes and saws and cannot even be used for firewood. Hundreds of birds nest in it and, all in all, it is perfectly worthless."

"Ah," answered Zhuangzi, "perhaps this troublesome tree of yours has some worth after all."

"But how can that be, you old faker!" cried the man.

"Think on it this way, honorable sir," says the sage, lightly stroking his whiskers. "You say the tree is of no use as lumber. It also cannot be chopped up for firewood. Think, then, of how useful that has been for the *tree*. It surely would never have attained its great height and size if it had been more useful to the carpenter or the woodcutter. Why, it would have been cut down long ago, would it not?

"The trees that have straight, true trunks or the ones that have easily cut limbs are never allowed to grow to maturity. They, by their very nature of usefulness, are killed very quickly and are not allowed to flourish into their true prime.

"This tree of yours, did you not say it shielded the whole yard from the harsh sunlight?"

"Why, yes," replied the man.

"Well then, go and sit in its cool shade and rest from your labors. Let your children climb and play in its crooked limbs. And as for the birds, would they not build their nests somewhere else, perhaps in your roof, if they did not have the tree to live in? Besides, try to listen to their singing with a different ear and perhaps their music will begin to delight you.

"So too, my friend, it is with men and women. Those who would make ostentatious display of their great worth are all too quickly used up and thrown aside. But those who appear useless in the eyes of the world are allowed to live out their lives in peace. Thus they may be able to provide some small nourishment to those around them."

It is just this concept of the value of worthlessness that marks Daoism as a unique philosophy. "Profit," says the *Daodejing*, "comes from what is there. Usefulness comes from what is not there." How different this way of thinking is from our modern world where one's worth depends on how bright one is or how attractive or how much one is able to accomplish, to produce!

In the face of this artificially high standard of worth, most people feel lacking. Our schools, our businesses, our streets are filled with people who feel they do not measure up. They do not feel they are worthy—of love, of respect, of happiness, of good fortune.

Zhuangzi describes the "true man of old" as one who "did not mind being poor. He took no pride in his achievements. He made no plans. Thus he could commit an error and not regret it. He could succeed without being proud."[1]

It is the intrinsic worthiness of being a human being, in all the most sublime and most inarticulate aspects, that gives us our worth, our special value. To look for it in outside achievements or in superficial and glamorous ways misses the point altogether. Our value as human beings, as emotional beings, as physical beings, as spiritual beings, resides deep within us, down in the place we all share, as children of the Dao.

Zhuangzi also tells us about a hunchbacked man named Shu. It seems the poor man was so deformed that his chin rested on his navel, his shoulders rose up over his head, his topknot pointed straight ahead, his organs were shoved together and his thigh bones were out of line with his hips. But by washing clothes and sewing, he was able to support himself.

Not content with that, he also winnowed and sifted grain and was able to make enough to support ten people. Also, when soldiers appeared in his village to press the men into service, they always passed over Shu. When work gangs were being formed for public works, he was exempt. And lastly, when the government gave out grain and wood to the needy, he always got more than anyone.

If this poor man, says Zhuangzi, was able to support himself so ably, how much easier should it be for those of us whose deformities are those of the mind!

He then tells us about Ai Tai To, the ugliest man in his district. He was said to be so ugly he would scare anyone under heaven, yet young women who saw him told their parents they would rather be his concubine than other men's wives! Because he always went along with whatever anyone else said, he was never in the position of leader or ruler over anyone else. And though he never left his village and knew only what happened there, everyone regarded him highly.

The Duke of Ai heard about this remarkable man and, deciding that he must find out his secret, summoned him to the court. Indeed Ai Tai To was extremely ugly—even hideous—yet there was something about the man that he liked, even trusted. After spending some time with him, the duke began giving Ai Tai To more and more responsibility in his government. At one point he offered him the position of chief minister. Bashfully, Ai Tai To hesitated as though he did not wish to take it. The duke became so ashamed of himself before this humble yet wise man that he gave him the entire government of his realm. But in a short time Ai Tai To disappeared, leaving the duke bereft and alone.

Shu and Ai Tai To, both deformed by the world's standards, yet so in synch with the Dao, were not only able to live out their lives in peace and contentment but also able to inspire in others a feeling of trust and even love. Could it be that they were able to realize the worthiness of the seemingly worthless?

> The mountain trees, in their usefulness,
> Ask to be cut down.
> The fat that is fed to the fire consumes itself.
> The cinnamon tree is tasty
> so they are cut down.
> The lacquer tree is useful
> So it is hacked apart.
> Everyone knows the use
> Of the useful.
> Where is the one who knows
> The usefulness of the useless?

We all want to be useful. We all want to be thought of as worthy—of love, of respect, perhaps even of attention and riches. We would like to think of ourselves as being useful to those around us—our families, our communities, the people we work with. But who actually measures usefulness? Who is it that sets up the scales of worthiness? Who *decides* who is worthy and who is not?

Daoism teaches us that each one of us—man, woman, child; black, white, red, brown or yellow—is a unique and miraculous being, and each of us deserves love, respect and the chance to express ourselves *as* ourselves, in the most unique and natural way we can. Only in this way can we personally determine our usefulness, our worthiness, our own special sense of who and what we are.

To overdo, to emphasize productivity, to oversharpen the blade is to invite disaster. When will the world acknowledge the worth of the mundane, the value of the ordinary, the utter preciousness of the commonplace?

This is the age of the celebrity, the superstar. No longer is a person satisfied with being merely competent or experienced at what she or he does, but now she or he must be the *best*, the most famous, the most successful, the most highly regarded.

Laozi, after writing the *Daodejing*, one of the most sublime and articulate books ever written, disappeared. He did not stay around to become the famous author, the great teacher, the powerful guru or religious leader. He did his work and left for the wilderness—and was never heard from again!

Although he was a great teacher and philosopher, Zhuangzi, too, preferred to remain a simple man. He tells the story about Hsu Yu, a fellow of such great wisdom that the Emperor Yao himself offered to step down from the dragon throne in his favor. Hsu Yu was so disgusted when he heard the offer that he not only refused but immediately ran to the river to wash out his ears! While he was there a boy came by, driving a team of oxen to the river to drink. The boy asked Hsu Yu why he was washing his ears out so thoroughly. Hsu Yu told him that the emperor had offered to abdicate the throne to him, which made him feel so dirty he had to run right down to the river and wash out his ears!

Upon hearing this the boy started driving his oxen out of the water. Hsu Yu asked him why he was driving his animals out of the river when they had not finished drinking yet. The boy replied, "The filth from your ears is dirtying the river water. Do you think I want my oxen to drink that?"

Daoism also gives close attention to cycles, those times when one is ahead, only the next day to be behind. One day everything goes well, the next, nothing works out. One day you are famous, beloved by the world, the next day you are a nobody. This is natural, say the Daoists; life is full of change. It encompasses each up and down and the all-too-brief moments in between. When we allow ourselves the space to be a nobody, to be willing to experience the down as well as the up days, we can come closest to being called men and women of Dao.

When we are willing to be worthless, we become worthy. As the ancient achieved ones explain, it is only in emptying ourselves of our mental and emotional baggage that we become fit to receive. This concept is illustrated by the story in the previous chapter of the somewhat arrogant gentleman whose teacup, like his mind, overflows.

The sage says to him, "Your mind, sir, is much like this teacup. I'm afraid it is already too full for me to be able to fit anything else into it. Else it will surely run over and spill everywhere."

So too must we be willing to empty our cups and become a *nobody*, to empty our minds and hearts of preconceived notions of knowledge and ideas of importance and accomplishment. To become a nobody is perhaps a greater accomplishment than to be a *somebody*. It seems in this day and age of mass communication and the fascination with celebrity that it is not so hard to become a somebody, if only for a day. The qualifications to become a somebody are getting slighter and slighter all the time. But to become a nobody—a happy, well-balanced nobody—ah, *that* is a challenge!

To be a nobody in this world of "wannabe" somebodys is an aspiration worthy of the highest student. To be a nobody is to say "yes" to the natural order of being. To be a nobody is to acknowledge that we are precious and perfect in our imperfection, worthy in our worthlessness. To be a nobody is to blend in with the world around us in perfect naturalness and simplicity. To be a nobody is to admit, to ourselves and to the world, that we are indeed linked with all the sages and, like them, we will continue to develop and grow and cultivate ourselves in a simple and natural manner. And lastly, to be a nobody is to redeem ourselves in our very emptiness, to be perfect vessels through which the Dao manifests itself continually.

Perhaps then we may be able to become as useful in our worthlessness as that ancient gnarled tree.

11

A Daoist Tea Ceremony

After hiking for four hours the day before, up and down many, many stone steps, we had arrived at the Tian Shi Dong, the Cave of the Heavenly Master, on Qingcheng Mountain, outside of Chengdu. It was here that Zhang Daoling, the founder of the first Daoist "church," the Heaven Master Sect, in the second century CE, did his cultivation in a local cave. The cave was later built into a temple complex, small by Chinese temple standards, but full of the *de* (spiritual energy) of the mountains.

Spending time in the shrine that contained the original cave of the master, one could not help but be impressed by the fortitude and strength it must have taken to hike all the way up here, before there were all those steps, when the mountain was full of wild animals, and spend time meditating in a cave, gathering the *de* of the mountain and circulating it into his own energy system. It must have taken a very fierce spirit indeed.

The following evening we gathered for a special Daoist tea ceremony, in a beautiful room off the temple teahouse. The front of the room contained a large painting of the character *dao*, where the tea master sat. To his right was a monk who took care of the incense for the ceremony. To his left was a nun who played the qin, an ancient stringed instrument, much loved by scholars, poets and recluses. Her lovely playing provided the background for our ceremony.

We sat on cushions on the floor; a small table in front of us held a large bowl of water with a teabag floating in it, a teacup with a lid and a small towel. Our able translator and guide, Sisi, translated what the master said.

There were five panels on the wall, explaining in poetry the steps of the tea ceremony. They consisted of a four-character phrase, describing each step of the tea ceremony, and a nine-character poem, describing the essence of each step, with a carving of the tea ceremony participant. I am indebted to my friend, Robert Santee, for the following translation of the panels.

Panel I
The participant, sitting on a cushion, is shown washing his hands in a basin while an attendant stands by with a cloth for drying:

> Fragrant/incense water cleans the hands.
> The water does not depend upon fragrance/incense,
> it depends upon cleansing.

Panel II
The participant, sitting on a cushion, is shown placing a lit stick of incense into an incense burner:

> Continuously burn the fragrance/incense of the mind/
>   heart.
> The fragrance/incense does not depend upon form,
> it depends on the mind/heart.

Panel III
The participant, sitting on a cushion, is shown meditating:

> Wash away the desires/dust of the mind/heart.
> The mind/heart does not depend upon understanding,
> it depends upon washing.

Panel IV
The participant, sitting on a cushion, is shown meditating:

> Sit in forgetfulness (*zuo wang*) maintaining (*shou*) stillness
>   (*jing*).
> Stillness does not depend upon circumstances,
> it depends upon forgetting (*wang*).

Panel V
The participant, sitting on a cushion, is shown looking into the teacup while holding the lid in his right hand and cradling the saucer with the teacup in his left hand:

> The three powers (heaven, earth and people) are united into
>   one.
> Heaven does not depend upon its vastness,
> it depends upon people.

"You may place your hands in your lap or on your leg," said the master. "Straighten up your body. Try your best to relax. Mr. Jou [a young acolyte] will help us fill up our tea. Miss Ma will play the qin for us." So began the ceremony.

"Daoists follow nature," said the master, "and so Daoists like tea because it comes from nature. The tea is the flavor of Dao. In the Way of Tea to drink tea and to meditate with tea is one part of Daoism. So right now just relax and don't worry about anything. Just let your body and your mind feel free and just enjoy the tea and enjoy the music.

"Today we are lucky to be together. This is a good place as it is in the mountains and quiet and it is a very good place to study Daoism. This is the best place to have tea and to combine it with Dao.

"Zhang Daoling is the master of Tian Shi Dong. He visited many places and many mountains in China, including some very famous Daoist mountains, but finally, he chose this mountain for his cultivation. So you can understand how nice and pure this mountain is. You can feel the special vitality here. People have been coming here since ancient times to cultivate themselves.

"The first thing is to put your hands into the bowl and wash them with the tea. Just feel relaxed and how you are in the middle of heaven and earth. When we put our hands into the bowl of tea we wash our hands and also our minds. The small bag in the bowl is a herbal blend from Qingcheng Mountain. These herbs are good for your skin and your health. Right now wash your hands three times and then use the towel to dry your hands.

"Put your hands together in front of your chest. Now is the time for some meditation. Remember not to worry about anything. Do not worry about things in the past or things in the future. Right now just follow the music and follow your breath and just let your body feel relaxed and comfortable."

After sitting in meditation for a short while, with the fragrant smell of incense filling the air and the harmonious sounds of the qin wafting out into the room, the master spoke again. We were told to use the tea to cleanse our heart and mind while the young acolyte went around the room filling our teacups with hot water.

Then we were told to use our left hand to lift the cup and our right hand to lift the cover and smell the fragrance of the tea, allowing it to fill our being with its rich fragrance. As in ancient times, Daoists believe that it is important to use the best water for brewing tea, with the best being pure spring water. Our tea was brewed with spring water from Qingcheng Mountain, gathered that very morning. Even the qin piece that the nun was playing was called *Peaceful Spring*.

"In ancient times the tea of Qingcheng Mountain was sent to the emperor in Beijing," said the master. "Right now we are drinking the tea that the emperor used to drink. By drinking this tea we unite ourselves with heaven and earth."

We were told to let the first sip of tea stay in our mouth for a few seconds before swallowing it, the better to let the essence of the tea permeate our entire being. We were then told to drink the tea in three swallows. Then the young monk came around again to fill up our cups with hot water.

"This ceremony will confer great blessings to us and the gods will follow our wish," said the master. "After drinking the second cup we will drink one more.

"In the *Daodejing*, it says that 'The Dao gives birth to the one, the one gives birth to the two, the two give birth to the three and the three give birth to the ten thousand beings.' This means that this ceremony will confer great blessings to you and everything will go well with you."

After drinking the second cup in the same way as the first, the young monk filled our cups a third time.

"We will now drink the tea for the third time," said the master. "First, breathe deeply three times to allow the fragrance of the tea to enter us and then drink it. This third time we drink the tea to thank heaven and the earth and nature as well as our parents who gave birth to us and took care of us."

We were then told we could drink more tea if we wished. The music stopped, the incense was put out and the master, after raising his enclosed fists in the Daoist salutation, left us to continue our tea ceremony in a more informal manner. In this way we were able to use this practice of drinking tea to reach the sublime heights of Daoist meditation and harmonization of our hearts and minds.

12

Making a Cup of Tea

In the Daoist Way of Tea, the drinking of tea, while it can be enjoyed for its own merits, can also be a very deep practice in itself. The art of drinking tea is represented by the gong fu tea ceremony. The term *gong fu* (often mistakenly pronounced kung fu) means any art that is mastered after much diligent practice. This can apply to anything from martial arts (called *wu shu* in China) to the art of serving and enjoying tea. Of course gong fu implies much experience and practice, so most of the time it is not possible for us to enter deeply into the experience right in the beginning. But with a little practice whole new worlds can open up to the student—whether of martial arts, painting, cooking or even serving and enjoying tea!

John Blofeld describes the Way of Tea as follows:

> the art of tea, like most traditional Chinese (and Japanese) arts, involves harmony among the Three Powers, heaven, earth and man. Heaven provides the sunshine, mist and rain

needed for growing the tea; earth provides soil
to nourish the tea plants, clay from which all
kinds of ceramic tea-things can be fashioned
and rocky springs overflowing with pure water
with which to brew the tea. To these man adds
the skills by which processed tea leaves, water
and ceramics are conjoined to create the fabric
of a seductive art.[1]

Of course we do not always have to perform a full-on gong fu tea
ceremony every time we want a cup of tea. To make a simple cup
of tea, heat water to just before it boils or else, if it does boil, let
it cool down for a few moments. Never pour boiling water over
Chinese tea, especially green tea. Now let it sit for two to three
minutes and then, if you are using a strainer, take it out of the tea.
(Some people like to throw the first infusion away before making
and drinking the second and third. You may notice a slight change
in flavor with various infusions.) If you are just putting the tea
leaves in the water, it would be best to strain them out before
drinking, although in China people often leave their leaves in the
cup or thermos all day and just keep adding more hot water. They
also tend to make their tea very strong. I would start with half a
teaspoon or even less in the beginning and then experiment with
how strong you like your tea.

Once, when I led a group to study qigong in Hangzhou, we
practiced every day by the beautiful West Lake at a teahouse there
in an old villa. They would serve us tea every morning but they
made it so strong that we would get dizzy after drinking it! We
had to ask them to please use fewer tea leaves. At the same time,
we did not ask for a discount, just fewer leaves. They were pretty
amused with the idea that we were asking for less but willing to
pay the same. They just did not get it that their tea was taking our
heads off!

If you are using a good quality tea you should be able to get several infusions from the same leaves. Try some different kinds of leaves and see which one appeals to you the most.

When I asked Master Wu in a personal interview on the best way to brew tea, he said:

> Actually you can boil it [the water] first, then the energy will be different. It will refine the energy. You boil it then allow it to cool down a little bit. Then you drink the tea until one third is left, then you add more water. Usually, with green tea, you can add more water three times.
>
> If the tea is good quality when you add water it will very quickly sink to the bottom of the cup. That is how you tell it is good quality. But green tea, if it is too old, the energy is gone and when you pour the water the leaves will float on the top. This means the energy is gone because the essential energy is descending. That is the way to drink green tea.
>
> The first pot, though, is not for drinking. It is for purification. First you very quickly pour the hot water onto the tea then pour it out, which purifies the tea itself. Then, on the second pot the flavor comes out. Then on the third maybe even better flavor.

If you are traveling to China you can get very good quality tea. Never use teabags, no matter what the packaging tells you. They always contain inferior quality tea and for just a little more money you can get a much better grade of tea. In China and in many quality teashops around the world you can get different grades of tea. I usually opt for the second to the top. It is not the most expensive and, unless you are a true connoisseur, you will not notice the difference. This tea can always be used for at least three infusions.

Every hotel or guesthouse room in China always has the ubiquitous thermos of hot water for making tea at any time, day or night. Recently I have seen a nifty little electric hot water heater, which heats up the water in minutes. Unfortunately, the tea provided is usually a low quality teabag. I always travel with my own tea or else use the tea I purchase there. I have even been known to take my own tea into the kitchen or dining room and ask them to use that instead of the tea they usually serve.

Two good shops I have found in the United States for high quality tea are Ten Ren Tea in San Francisco and The Tao of Tea in Portland, Oregon. If you are able to visit in person you will often be treated to a tasting of each tea in tiny cups. Or you can order a pot of tea and have it prepared and presented to you in the traditional manner. The Tao of Tea has several locations in Portland, including one in a traditional-style teahouse in the beautiful and elegant Chinese Garden in downtown Portland. There you get to sit by the window overlooking the pond and gaze out over the Suzhou-style garden there. You will have an opportunity to sample teas from all over the world there. Just tell them Solala sent you! See the section on "Sources for Tea" for contact details and a few more choices in the United States and elsewhere.

If you are traveling to China you can visit teashops in any city. Of course it is even more fun to go to a traditional teahouse and be regaled with storytelling or musicians. There you can sit and drink tea and nibble on tea snacks for hours for very low cost.

If you visit a teashop in China and do not speak Chinese here are a few pointers. When you enter, greet the people there with a hearty "Ni Hao" (hello). Then ask if they have any Dragon Well tea (my personal favorite and a very famous green tea) by saying "Ni yo bu yo Lung Jing cha?"

Most likely they will and will answer "Wo yo." Then they will show you various grades. To ask how much it is say "Duoxiou?"

This is the part you will need a pocket calculator for unless you are good at doing math in your head. The exchange rate fluctuates so you will need to know what it is when you arrive in China.

Most of the time they will ask you to sit down and offer you some taste tests of various teas or grades of tea. Take your time and relax. This will be an opportunity to slow down from a busy day of sightseeing or shopping and spend some time with fellow tea people. Even if you do not speak Chinese, you will be amazed by how much you can say with nods and smiles. Be sure and say "Xie xie," pronounced shie shie (thank you), when you leave. You can also say "Zai jian" (goodbye).

If you visit the Hangzhou area, famed for its tea gardens, be sure to visit a tea plantation and get a chance to see how they process the tea after picking (it is especially fun to see the guys stirring the tea leaves in a hot wok with their bare hands). There is even a tea museum there.

In Hangzhou I was told that it is best to store tea in the refrigerator in order to keep it fresh. Good quality tea will last longer than lower quality but one year is the most you should store any kind of tea. After that it loses most of its flavor as well as its qi.

As far as what to brew the tea in, you can use either a ceramic cup with a ceramic filter and cover, found in most Asian grocery stores or gift shops, or a plain ceramic cup. In China many people use glass jars which, though not as pleasing aesthetically, do allow one to view the brewing leaves in a nice way.

The teapot should never be metal, especially aluminum, which is a health hazard. The best thing to use would be a small ceramic teapot. Kenneth Cohen, in the tea section of his excellent book on qigong, *The Way of Qigong*, says:

> The very best is Chinese Yi Xing Ware, from the town of Yi Xing in Jiangsu Province. The Yi Xing red clay has been used to make teapots since at least 1500. The pots are generally

unglazed to display the subtle earth tones of the clay and to allow seasoning of the pot. They hold the warmth, flavor, and qi of tea like no other utensil.[2]

One of the most important things to remember, when embarking on the Way of Tea, is to slow down, take your time and not only brew the tea in the right way, but also, most importantly, drink it in the right way. This means not drinking it while driving down the road, talking on your cell phone or listening to the radio. Instead, allow yourself enough time to really enjoy your tea. You can curl up with a good book or spend time with your friends or loved ones or just sit and enjoy the tea for itself.

Notes

1.   Blofeld, *The Chinese Art of Tea*, p.xiii.
2.   Cohen, *The Way of Qigong*, p.315.

13

A Gong Fu Tea Ceremony

> The best state of mind in which to drink tea is one of deep meditation. The second best is while looking at a beautiful landscape or listening to music. The third best is during stimulating conversation. In all cases it is necessary to aspire towards a quiet and tranquil frame of mind. (Paichang, Chinese Chan master)[1]

A classical Chinese tea ceremony is usually called a *gong fu* tea ceremony. The term gong fu means "preparing with care" or "skill that comes with practice" and can actually be applied to any art, including *wu shu* or Chinese martial arts (often called kung fu in the West). It can include painting or music or anything else that is done with care and appreciation.

In China and Japan the tea ceremony is a way to transcend the mundane world and share a moment of timeless time with friends. If approached with the right attitude and graceful timing, the tea ceremony can be a bridge to another world—one of refinement and harmony.

As John Blofeld describes it:

> Getting the fullest satisfaction from the tea art requires a special sate of mind analogous to what Buddhists mean by awareness. This is achieved by attending to the responses of all six senses: hearing, smelling, tasting, seeing, touching and consciousness. Once it has become habitual, there is no need to bestow further thought on it.[2]

The utensils used in a gong fu tea ceremony are as follows:

- A kettle for heating the water. In the old days this was heated with coal or wood, but most people now use a stove or electric burner to heat the water.
- One or two small clay pots. These are for brewing the tea and then serving it. It is best if one can use the *yixing* clay pots for these two. These are made especially for this purpose and are made of very porous clay, which absorbs the flavors of the tea and enhances the taste of tea brewed in them. (Note: It is important never to use soap or detergent to clean these pots as they will take on the flavor of the cleaning agent. Just clean them with hot water and let them air dry.)
- Teacups. You can use either one or two different types of cups (*cha bei*). The cup that you drink out of is usually very small, only big enough for two or three mouthfuls. A small cylindrical cup is also used for enjoying the aroma of the tea and is called a fragrance cup.
- A tea tray. This is a hollow square tray made of wood or earthenware. The pots and cups are placed on the top and when the water is poured over them it goes into holes in the surface of the tray and then into the bottom of the tray, to be discarded at the end of the ceremony.

- A wooden tea spoon or scoop. Also a set of wooden tweezers or tongs can be used to handle the hot cups in the beginning of the ceremony.

These tea sets can now be found very easily in any Chinatown in a large city or online from various tea websites.

The gong fu tea ceremony is usually done with *oolong* or red teas but can really be done with any green tea. The ceremony itself can be as serious or ritualistic as you like. It can also be a very informal and relaxed time between friends.

To begin, boil the water. Actually one usually either takes the water off just before it comes to a boil, or one can boil the water and then let it sit a moment to cool down slightly. In any case, you never pour fully boiling water onto the tea.

Pour the hot water into the pot as well as over the outside to heat it up and also the cups to heat them up and prepare them for the tea. If you have the traditional tongs, use them to pick up each small cup and pour the water in it into the next cup and so on. Pour the water onto the outside of the cups as well. When you are done, pour the water from the cups as well as from the pot into the tea tray.

Add tea leaves, using the wooden spoon or bamboo scoop, to the first pot and then fill it with water. This first infusion is usually poured off after a very short amount of time. This removes any dust from the leaves and is sometimes called "washing the leaves."

Often the tea leaves themselves are passed around to all the participants, so that they can see and smell the tea before it is brewed. As Chinese tea comes in a wide variety of colors, shapes and smells, this can be quite interesting.

Then fill the teapot once again, being sure to pour more hot water over the outside of the pot. This time, after roughly 30–60 seconds, the tea is poured into the cylindrical fragrance cup. The small drinking cup is placed on top of the fragrance cup and flipped over so that the tea is poured into the drinking cup. Then the fragrance cup is raised by the participants to inhale the aroma of the tea. The tea is then drunk, not in one gulp, but slowly, savoring the flavor, aroma and color of the tea. You can, of course, dispense with the fragrance cup. If you do, be sure to have everyone stop and admire the color and inhale the subtle aroma of the tea before they drink it.

As my friend Zhongxian Wu says:

> The way to hold the cup is also different than usual tea drinking. You use just three fingers, which represent Heaven, Earth and Humanity. Also, you hold it so that your lao gong point on your palm connects with your middle dantian in your chest so that you are connected through your heart. It is a spiritual connection. Then you drink and you are tasting it; your nose smells it also at the same time.[3]

Depending on the tea, this process can be done again for three or four or even more times. Each time the tea is left to infuse a bit longer. Good quality tea can be infused up to six times in this way. You can use just one teapot or you can use another one to store the tea in once it is brewed.

Some tea people take a great deal of care in how they pour the water into the teapot—such as pouring the water in a circular way into the pot or in moving the hot water kettle up and down three times as they pour. This is like bowing three times at an altar and denotes respect.

Always offer the teacup to each participant using both hands. This is another way to show respect. As a matter or fact, traditionally minded Chinese people will always offer anything, even money or their business card, with both hands. It is also respectful to receive whatever is being offered with both hands. This is true for Tibet too.

Unlike the Japanese Zen tea ceremony, the Chinese gong fu tea ceremony is informal and the participants may talk about almost anything under the sun, enjoying each other's company, while at the same time allowing for some restraint. The main idea is to leave one's cares and woes behind, if only for a short time, and just enjoy the company of good friends and good tea!

Light snacks may also be offered and sometimes the tea is poured into clear glass cups, the better to appreciate the color of the tea.

It is important to feel a sense of harmony and peacefulness when serving or drinking tea in this way. It is not necessary to go into some sort of trance but just be able to feel "free and easy." To practice the Way of Tea in this way we become connected to the five elements, the *wu hsing*. The tea comes from the element wood. The pottery comes from the earth. Heat or fire is used to bring the water to boil. The last element in Chinese thought is often translated as metal but in the old texts it is described as gold. The gold is what you bring to the gong fu tea ceremony. It is also the fellowship you create by sharing tea with others in this way. So here we have a simple yet heartful ceremony, one which brings all five elements into play and into balance.

Let us end with another quote from John Blofeld:

> Taking part in a tea session is a way of awakening to the Here and Now. To enjoy such subtle pleasures as the hiss and bubble of a kettle, the small white clouds of steam, the harmony of thoughtfully chosen utensils, the colour, flavour and aroma of the tea, one must resolutely banish cares (instead of allowing them to gnaw the mind like rats) and keep one's mind and senses focused on what lies to hand. This art, besides being delightful in itself, is a great deal cheaper than most other forms of therapy.[4]

Notes

1. Quoted in Theresa Cheung (2007) *Tea Bliss*, p.156.
2. John Blofeld (1985) *The Chinese Art of Tea*, p.130.
3. Personal interview.
4. Blofeld, *The Chinese Art of Tea*, p.163.

14

The Health Benefits of Tea

Tea is an addiction, but an addiction different from all others. It is milder, a habit relatively easily broken. It is more universal. Most unusually, it is good for the addict. And it is .largely unnoticed both to those addicted and to others. Indeed, the conquest of the world by tea has been so successful that we have forgotten that it has happened at all. Tea has become like water or air, something that many of us take for granted.[1]

As previously mentioned, tea began its illustrative career as a medicinal drink. It was only later on that it became a popular drink for every day, and as the Chinese do, every hour of the day! Even so, the health benefits from drinking tea are myriad.

The first is that it is made from boiling water. In many parts of the world drinking water is unsafe and the source of many diseases. The simple practice of boiling the water before drinking it kills many of the microbes and parasites that would be passed on if it were not boiled. The substances found in tea have also been found to destroy the bacteria that causes diseases such as cholera, typhoid and both amoebic and bacillary dysentery.

As the Macfarlanes point out:

> The great surge of population, economy and culture that occurred in China after about 700 AD, reaching its climax in the glories of the Sung [song] dynasty, has never really been explained. Clearly, there was political unification and improved technology and communications. All this was important. Yet it is worth noting that however much economic and political efficiency was improved, it would have been to no avail if China had suffered the normal trap of rising death rates. If the people who lived very close together, whether in the growing cities, towns or crowded countryside, had grown rice and drunk unboiled water, they would increasingly have suffered from dysentery and other waterborne diseases. Their strength and their numbers would have dwindled, and large numbers of infants would have died from enteric diseases.[2]

The health benefits of tea have been known for centuries. A herbal manual by Li Shih Chen, published in 1578, states that tea will "promote digestion, dissolve fats, neutralize poisons in the digestive system, cure dysentery, fight lung disease, lower fevers, and treat epilepsy." In addition, "tea was also thought to be an effective astringent for cleaning sores and recommended for washing the eyes and mouth."[3]

The traditional view of tea drinking includes the claims that it can:

- increase blood flow to all parts of the body;
- stimulate clear thinking and mental alertness;

- speed the elimination of alcohol and other harmful substances (fats and nicotine, for example) from the bodily organs;
- increase the body's powers of resistance to a wide range of diseases;
- accelerate the metabolism and the intake of oxygen by the bodily organs;
- prevent tooth decay;
- benefit and brighten the eyes;
- assist the digestion;
- banish fatigue or fits of depression, raising the spirits and inducing a general feeling of well-being;
- prolong the life span of the individual.[4]

What is it about this humble plant that it is able to offer so much to our health and well-being? This is in large part due to the presence of a number of ingredients including vitamins such as vitamin C (protecting the immune system), B6 (helping to balance metabolism), B1 and B2 (releasing energy from the food we eat and also maintaining thyroid function). It also contains two important minerals—potassium, which helps maintain fluid levels in the body and keeps the heart beating, and manganese, which is essential for body development and bone growth. It also contains fluoride which can help fight tooth decay.

One of the most important and exciting ingredients in tea are polythenols., which can help prevent bad breath. Polythenols are naturally occurring compounds in tea that have a strong anti-oxidant quality. Green tea has much more of these than black tea, because it is not as processed. Green tea has been proven to have two hundred times the antioxidant levels than vitamin E. This antioxidant quality of tea may play a part in preventing certain cancers such as pancreas, prostate, colon, esophagus and mouth.

These powerful antioxidants counteract fatty deposits in the arteries, which can keep cholesterol down and also prevent hardening of the arteries. One study by Harvard Medical School said that drinking one cup of tea can cut the risk of having a heart attack by 44 percent. This again would be green tea we are talking about here.

Oxidation is a process of molecular DNA damage, which is caused when unstable and toxic molecules known as free radicals develop in our body. These free radicals have the power to seriously damage our system and can cause immune system weakness, chronic illness, organ disease and overall physical deterioration. An unhealthy lifestyle of junk food, tobacco and alcohol abuse (even second-hand smoke) and other environmental stresses all contribute to the growth of free radicals in our body. The polyphenols in tea bind with the free radicals and cancel their damaging effects.

There are also many other minerals contained in green tea besides the two we already mentioned. Others are chromium, magnesium, calcium, sodium, phosphorus, strontium, cobalt and nickel. In addition, green tea contains amino acids, the building blocks of proteins, including aspartic acid, glutamic acid, glycine, glutamine, tyrosine, alanine, valine, arginine, tryptophan and proline. It also contains an amino acid, theanine, that is unique to tea; theanine contains about half the amino acids in green tea and plays a role in the biosynthesis of polyphenols. Green tea extract seems to enhance the effectiveness of some anti-cancer medications while minimizing their side effects.[5]

Here is another interesting study on tea and skin cancer.

> Scientists are demonstrating amazing success studying tea's preventive properties against skin cancer. At Rutgers University, laboratory mice were separated into four groups, each drinking only one of four kinds of tea for thirty-one weeks: green or black, both regular and decaffeinated. A control group drank only water. During the study the mice were exposed to two carcinogens known to cause cancer. The tea-drinking mice

developed 70 percent to 90 percent fewer skin cancers than the control group. Green and black tea were equally effective, and the decaffeinated teas showed only slightly reduced results.[6]

There are also studies and lab tests that cover a wide variety of other conditions such as inflammatory bowel disease, diabetes, Alzheimer's, stroke, cardiovascular health, bacterial and fungal infections, iron overload disorders, dealing with stress hormones, and help with a wide range of cancers.

In the *wu xing* or five element theory of Chinese medicine, the five different flavors affect different organs. The flavor of tea, bitter, is the one connected to the heart and heart health. Eisai, the Japanese monk who did the most to introduce tea to Japan, wrote:

> the health of the five human organs is strengthened through the plentiful intake of the five flavours they respectively enjoy. ... But whilst people absorb the four flavours of sharp, sour, sweet and salty, the bitter flavour necessary for the heart is unpleasant and cannot be taken in. This is the reason why Japanese hearts are afflicted and Japanese lives short. We are fortunately able to learn from the people of the continent and we must make our hearts healthy absorbing the bitter flavour of the tea.[7]

All of this is beyond the scope of this book. There are many excellent books on the health benefits of tea such as *The Green Tea Book* by Lester A. Mitscher and Victoria Dolby. And there are more studies being done all the time. Suffice it to say that tea, especially green tea, more than lives up to its reputation for health benefits going back to Shen Nong and beyond.

A word or two about caffeine. Of course there is caffeine in all tea, especially in black tea. Caffeine is a stimulant to the central nervous system and is found in many plants, including tea, coffee and cacao. There is much less caffeine in tea, however, than in coffee, especially in green tea.

> The practitioners of the forms of religion that spread in China—Taoism and especially Buddhism—were particularly attracted by a plant that could help meditation by increasing mental concentration and staving off sleep. So much did Buddhists come to appreciate this new elixir that, in certain sects, tea-drinking was elevated to one of the four ways of concentrating the mind, alongside walking, feeding fish and sitting quietly in thought.[8]

Caffeine has been used in this way for hundreds of years. The British Pharmaceutical Codex of 1923 describes the effects of tea in this way:

> The acting on the central nervous system is mainly on that part of the brain connected with physical functions. It produces a condition of wakefulness and increased mental activity. The interpretation of sensory impressions is more perfect and correct and thought becomes clearer and quicker. ...Caffeine facilitates the performance of all kinds of physical work, and actually increases the total work which can be obtained from a muscle.[9]

Of course, one can overdo caffeine, with the effect of overloading the nervous system. But by not making the tea too strong this can be easily avoided. Another option is to pour out the first infusion, as is done in the gong fu tea ceremony, which contains most of the caffeine.

The amount of caffeine in tea is much less than coffee. For instance, in an 8 ounce serving of brewed coffee we find 60–160 mg of caffeine. In a comparable serving of black tea we get 20–90 mg. Oolong tea is 10–45 mg and green tea is 6–30mg. So you can see that the caffeine contained in most teas is much less than in coffee. This, along with all the other added benefits of tea, makes it an ideal source of caffeine.

Another thing that determines the amount of caffeine that is found in any one cup of tea is also highly influenced by the type of tea, the way it was processed, how much is used at any one time, and how long it is infused. Most teas should be infused for only 2–3 minutes, especially green tea.

So as we have seen, not only is tea the beverage of choice for the artist, the poet, the sage and the monk but also its health benefits are enormous. It is in the very spirit of tea that we find many of its most important benefits. As my friend Frank Hadley Murphy writes in his excellent book, *The Spirit of Tea*:

> Creation speaks to us through all its manifestations, if we are willing to listen. Science may be able to quantify tea's effects on our bodies, but it cannot quantify its effects on our souls, and that's exactly where tea shares with us her deepest mysteries.
>
> Her sobering humility resonates with our own original nature.
>
> Her subtle beauty reminds us of the beauty of our own perfection.
>
> Her soothing calm cuts through our spiritual materialism and brings us to a state of grace.
>
> She wakens in us not only the intellect of the mind but more importantly, the intelligence of the heart.
>
> Tea calls to our deepest selves and invites us to celebrate with it.[10]

Notes

1. Alan Macfarlane and Iris Macfarlane (2004) p.31. Published in North America as *The Empire of Tea: The Remarkable History of the Plant That Took Over the World* by The Overlook Press. Published in the United Kingdom as *Green Gold: The Empire of Tea*, by Ebury Press. Reprinted by permission of The Overlook Press and Random House Group Ltd. All rights reserved.

2. Macfarlane and Macfarlane, *The Empire of Tea*, p.168.

3. Ibid. Both quotes from p.48.

4. John Blofeld (1985) *The Chinese Art of Tea*, p.156.

5. Mitscher and Dolby, *The Green Tea Book*.

6. Jill Yates (2005) *Tales of a Tea Leaf*, p.96.

7. Macfarlane and Macfarlane, *Green Gold: The Empire of Tea*, p.53.

8. Ibid., p.44.

9. Ibid., p.256.

10. Frank Hadley Murphy (2008) *The Spirit of Tea*, p.21.

15
Types of Tea

There are five types of tea—green, white, oolong, red (or what is called black in the West) and pu-erh—though they all come from the same tea plant, *camellia sinensis*. The main difference is how the tea leaves are processed after picking, which can make a huge difference to what kind of tea is produced.

Green tea is usually the least processed. Red or black tea is the most processed, after pu-erh, which is in a class of its own. (More on this later.) The way the tea is processed can also alter its chemical composition and how our bodies respond to it.

The picking of the tea is usually done at dawn, just before the sun comes up. Traditionally, it is done by girls or young women, as their small hands and fingers are just the right size for clipping off the right amount of leaf and bud. For high grade tea only the top two leaves and bud are taken. Sometimes it is just a bud and one leaf, or for some rare and exotic teas, only the bud is taken. It can take many thousands of these to add up to a pound of tea!

Often the women sing traditional songs or else joke and gossip while they pick the leaves and toss them into a bamboo basket on their back. In some places, especially in Japan, the tea is plucked by machine, but that usually produces a lower quality of tea.

After the leaves are picked they are spread out onto baskets, tables or trays to dry or "wither," thereby losing a great deal of their moisture. Then they are bruised or rolled, either by hand or by machine. This also brings out the flavor and aroma of the tea.

This begins the process of oxidation, often mistakenly called fermentation. It also releases some of the juices of the leaf. In this step the tea is "rolled," sometimes by machine but more often by hand if a high quality tea is to be the result. This process is to break the membrane of the leaves, to release the chemical substances called catechins and the enzyme polyphenolase, which starts the oxidation process.

If the tea is to become green tea, the process of oxidation is very short. If, on the other hand, the tea is to be red or black tea it will take many hours of oxidation. The leaves are spread out in a temperature-controlled environment. The leaves absorb oxygen for several hours, with the leaves themselves turning red around the edges or even black.

The next step is firing. This is when the leaves are either dried in a slow heat in a drying chamber or, as in some green teas such as Lung Jing, dried in a wok by hand. This stops the enzyme action, sterilizes the leaves and stops the oxidation process. It further dehydrates the leaves so that they can be stored without going bad. This is also when some teas are rolled into small balls or pills such as the well-known gunpowder tea.

For green tea, the rolling or breaking of the membrane is not done. The oxidation process is also not done. This instills a more subtle flavor of the green tea in contrast to the black or oolong tea.

If the tea is to become oolong (Black Dragon) tea then the oxidation process is done for about half the amount of time for black tea. After the leaves are picked they are laid out to dry for 8–24 hours. Next they are tossed in baskets to bruise the edges of the leaves. Then the leaves are steamed in order to neutralize the enzymes and stop any more oxidation.

Oolong tea takes the most skill at handcrafting it. It tends to be more aromatic and for this reason is the one most often used in a gong fu tea ceremony. There are major oolong tea competitions in China, with the winning tea going for up to $20,000 a pound!

White tea consists of just the unopened bud of certain varieties of the tea plant along with a few young leaves, mostly found in the Fujian province. These versions of the tea plant produce buds that, after processing, are covered with a fine white hair. This produces a tea that is very delicate in flavor, even more so than green tea.

Pu-erh is often made from green and black tea, mixed together and allowed to ferment. It is then compressed into cakes, much like in ancient times. These cakes, if processed correctly, can last for many years. It is a very strong, earthy taste and not for everyone.

Another type of tea is the fragrant variety, such as jasmine tea. In this process green tea is mixed with jasmine flowers and left for 10–12 hours so that the scent of the jasmine flowers is fully taken in by the tea leaves. For the very high grades of jasmine tea this process may be done an additional four or five times.

Here are some of the most famous and delectable teas.

Green teas
Lung Jing (Dragon Well)
This famous tea is primarily grown in the Hangzhou area in Zhejiang province. It is meticulously prepared using traditional methods from tender tea leaves. The finished tea leaves have a flat and smooth appearance. The four outstanding unique characteristics of Dragon Well tea are its green jade color, its orchid-like smell, the sparrow's tongue shape of its dried

leaves, and its fresh taste and semi-sweet aftertaste. This tea was mentioned by Lu Yu in his famous work on tea.

Purple Bamboo

The name comes from the tea's plump and pointy buds which bear resemblance to bamboo. This tea is grown on Mount Guzhu, China. From the Tang dynasty to the Ming dynasty, a span of about 600 years, this tea was consumed by the emperor's royal family. This tea is harvested around April when the stalks are pink and the buds are white. This tea is made from young tea leaves. The finished tea leaves have a flat, thin and uniform look with a green color. Tea made from these leaves has a strong taste with body and pleasant, slightly sweet and clean aftertaste.

Gunpowder

Gunpowder Green Tea derives its name from the shape of its finished leaves. The very dark green tea leaves have been rolled into little pellets which look like gunpowder. Good Gunpowder Tea uses older tea leaves unlike other varieties of green tea. Tea steeped from Gunpowder has a dark golden color and a roasted or toasted taste with a strong flavor. This tea, because of how tightly rolled it is, can be stored much longer than other green teas.

Houjicha Green Tea

This is a Japanese green tea that is pan fried or oven roasted to stop the oxidation process. The steeped tea has a golden brown color, a moderately baked aroma, a mildly fresh taste with sweet undertones and a smooth aftertaste with roasted undertones.

Dragon and Phoenix Needles (Pan Long Yin Hao)

This tea uses the highest quality young and tender tea leaves grown in the high mountains of China. When it is harvested, great care is taken to choose only the freshly blossomed leaves and its bud of about 1.5 centimeters in length. Only leaves harvested in the early spring are used for this tea. The baking process uses charcoal as the fuel instead of the more typical gas. The finished tea leaves have a clean plump look with white touches, thicker and plumper than others with very few stems. When steeped, these leaves produce a tea that has a light pleasing smell with a smooth taste and strong aftertaste. The hue of the tea is a bright greenish yellow. Some connoisseurs say that the brewed tea leaves look like dancing dragons.

Chun Mee (Ming Mei)
This is another popular green tea. Also called "precious eyebrow tea," it has a dusty appearance and is generally more acidic and less sweet than other green teas. It was originally produced only in the Jiangxi province, but is now grown elsewhere. The processing of this tea demands great skill in the rolling of the leaves to create the unique shape of the precious eyebrow.

Bi Lo Chun
Also known as Green Snail Spring, this is a tea that is famous for its snail-like appearance. The other special thing about this tea is that it is grown among peach, plum and apricot trees so that it takes on some of the fragrance of the fruit. When picking, only one leaf at a time is plucked.

Xinyang Maojian
Grown in the misty mountains of the Xinyang area. Hand rolled, this tea is known for its fresh aroma and subtle aftertaste.

Sencha
This is a traditional Japanese green tea with tightly rolled, needle-shaped leaves. It is picked in early spring after the leaves have developed their balance of sweetness and astringency. The liquor is bright in color, with a taste somewhat reminiscent of seaweed. True Sencha differs in character from most Chinese-style green

teas not only with its sleek, dark green appearance but also its higher green notes compared to nuttier, vegetal notes.

Matcha

This is the powdered tea used in Japan for the traditional Zen tea ceremony. The preparation of Matcha starts several weeks before harvest, when the tea bushes are covered to prevent direct sunlight. This slows down growth, turns the leaves a darker shade of green and causes the production of amino acids that make the resulting tea sweeter. Only the finest tea buds are hand picked. After harvesting, if the leaves are rolled out before drying as usual, the result will be *gyokuro* (Jewel Dew) tea. However, if the leaves are laid out flat to dry, they will crumble somewhat and become known as *tencha*. Tencha can then be deveined, destemmed and stone ground to the fine, bright green, talc-like powder known as Matcha. It can take up to an hour to grind 30 grams of matcha.

Hyson

The leaves that are used to make this tea are thick and yellow-green and are twisted into long, thin shapes in its processing. It is one of the more pungent tasting of the green teas.

Jin Chu

This tea, also known as Orchid Snow, is grown on the sunny peaks of Shao Xing and is the one that our scholar from the Ming dynasty, Zhang Dai, was so in love with. It is a tea that is grown in a much sunnier area than usual for tea and so it is called sun-fused. Its leaves are long, white and slender and the tea is very full bodied and sweet.

Black (red) teas

Keemun Black Tea

This tea is regarded by many as China's finest black tea. The name Keemun comes from the county Qimen in Anhui province.

Keemun Black Tea has a reddish brown color with a roasted and strong, sweet aroma. The taste is sweet and smooth.

Yunnan Black Tea

Yunnan is a region in China known for producing excellent black tea. Yunnan is famous for its fat golden buds. Tea has a reddish brown color. The aroma is strong, sugary and floral with a slight roasted undertone.

Golden Monkey Black Tea

Golden Monkey Black Tea is grown in the Fujian province in China. Fujian is a region known for producing excellent black tea with golden buds. The brewed tea has a reddish brown hue with a sugary aroma with floral and roasted undertones. The taste is smooth with sweet undertones, with a clean and refreshing aftertaste.

Earl Grey

Earl Grey tea is harvested from the central mountains of Sri Lanka and scented with the oil of bergamot. Grown at elevations over 5000 feet above sea level, this high quality tea is carefully selected and scented to exacting standards. Tea brewed from Earl Grey has a clear deep red hue. The taste and aroma is rich with sweet citrus undertones and lingering briskness. In the early nineteenth century, a Chinese nobleman presented this tea to the British prime minister, Earl Grey, hence the name of this tea. Earl Grey is one of the most popular black teas in the world and may be enjoyed hot or cold with or without sugar, cream and lemon.

English Breakfast

English Breakfast tea is a special blend of high quality black tea grown and selected from the central mountains of Sri Lanka. It has a clear dark red hue. The taste is pure with a strong malt-like aftertaste and the aroma is lightly sweet. This tea can be enjoyed with cream or lemon.

Lapsong Souchong
Lapsong Souchong is a black tea with a distinctive flavor created by the smoking procedure. Legend claims that the special smoking procedure was discovered by accident. During the Qing dynasty, a group of soldiers occupied a tea factory for one night. The factory contained fresh tea leaves to be processed for the next day's market. By the time the soldiers vacated the factory and the workers returned to process the leaves, there was not enough time to dry the leaves the usual way. The workers lit fires of pine wood to quicken the drying. By the next morning, the tea was ready to be sold and was discovered to have a smoked pine flavor which enhanced the tea. Nowadays the leaves are first dried over fires of pine or cypress wood. Then they are placed into wooden barrels to ferment. The leaves are fried again and placed over smoking pine fires to absorb the smoke flavor. Lapsong Souchong, a favorite of Sherlock Holmes and other fictional Britons, can be enjoyed with or without milk and sugar.

Oolong teas
Scarlet Robe Oolong
Also known as Da Hong Pao, Scarlet Robe consists of fine oolong harvested from the Wuyi Mountains in Fujian, China. The name originates from an emperor who was cured by this tea and hung his scarlet robes onto the bush to commemorate it. The steeped tea has a dark orange hue, a slightly roasted aroma with floral undertones and a slightly roasted flavor.

Tie Guan Yin
This tea is from Anxi, China, a town in the southern part of Fujian province. Anxi is famous for producing and growing top quality Tie Guan Yin. The steeped tea has a golden yellow hue, a mellow floral aroma with slight roasted undertones, a brief smooth initial flavor, and a lightly sweet, fresh aftertaste which lasts long after the sip.

High Mountain Oolong
Hand picked and painstakingly crafted at the famed Shan Ling Xi Mountain in Taiwan, this oolong is jade green to light golden in color. The body is deep and full with a finish that is silky smooth and sweet. Take a moment to look at the steeped leaves and note the "two leaves and a bud" sets and the deep, thick, healthy glow of the green leaves.

Shui Jin Gui
This is a very characteristic Wuyi Oolong tea, whose name literally means Golden Marine Turtle. The tea produces a bright green color when steeped and is much greener than most other Wuyi Oolong teas.

Bai Ji Guan
This is a very light Wuyi tea. It is named after a rooster who gave up its life while protecting a child. Legend has it that the name of this marvelous tea (White Cockscomb) was given by a monk in memorial of a courageous rooster that sacrificed his life while protecting his baby from an eagle. Touched by the display of courage and love, the monk buried the rooster and, from that spot, the Bai Ji Guan tea bush grew. Bai Ji Guan's wonderful complex taste makes it one of the best oolong in the world. Unlike most Wuyi teas, the leaves of this tea are yellowish rather than green or brown.

Pu-erh tea

Pu-erh tea is a famous and popular beverage in Canton province and southwestern China. It is a fermented tea. When brewed Pu-erh tea has a dark reddish color with a strong, full and earthy taste. Water at boiling point should be used for steeping.

Jasmine tea

Jasmine tea is a famous tea made from Green or Pouchong (Chinese Green) tea leaves that are scented with jasmine flowers. The jasmine flowers are harvested during the day and stored in a cool place until night. During the night, the flowers bloom with full fragrance. The flowers are layered over the tea leaves during the scenting process. The quality of jasmine tea is determined by the quality of green tea used as its base and the effectiveness of the scenting.

16
Tea Time

The old man rose early in the morning, as he usually did, in order to catch the first rays of the sun. He stood in front of his humble hut and, eyes closed, energy gates open, allowed the warm flood of sunlight to descend from the heavens and flow gently down his body.

Then, taking up a small pot, he went out amidst his garden, gathering dew for his first cup of tea of the day. Slowly and gently he dipped each leaf towards his small pot, allowing the small drops of dew to flow into it. He did this many times, as many times as it took to fill the pot. After that he built up a small fire and put the pot on to warm. He sat there awhile, waiting for the water to heat up, almost to boiling point, but not quite.

When he judged it ready, he took from a shelf a small bamboo canister of tea. It was Lung Jing, Dragon Well, the first of the season. It had cost him quite a lot of money but he had such simple tastes in everything else that it was well worth it.

He poured the dew into his small teapot and let the leaves sit in the water for a few moments. Any more and it would have been a waste of the precious tea leaves. He poured the tea into an unglazed cup. He raised it to his face and, sniffing deeply, allowed the fragrant aroma of the tea to fill his head. Then he took a small sip and held it in his mouth for a moment before he swallowed. It was good and he was glad he had spent the money for the best quality but one. (The highest quality was, of course, reserved for the emperor.)

He sat there, slowly savoring his tea and watching the world wake up around him. He felt his own body and mind waking up along with it, as the tea did its gentle work. He treasured these first moments of the day, when it was just himself and the world around him, sharing in this first cup of tea of the day.

He often had friends over in the evening. They would sit and drink tea together and talk about this and that. He always served his tea in simple earthen cups with little glaze. He had made them in his youth when he had made many things like this—pots, bowls, cups. Some of what he had made were very intricate, with colorful deep glazes—made for the aristocracy who loved such fancy things.

He had lived in the capital then and his life was full of comings and goings. It was so much simpler now. Of course he had enjoyed his life then, as he enjoyed his life now.

He held his teacup up to the sun and marveled at the tiny criss-crossing cracks that ran all along its sides, some of which had been there after its first firing and others which had shown up there with time. Like his own face, he thought, with its criss-crossing cracks and the deep furrows that time had cut there.

He built up the fire a little and brought some more water almost to the boiling point and filled his little teapot again. The leaves were good for at least three steepings. Good quality tea was like that.

He sat and drank and ruminated and breathed deeply; after a while he went over to the shelf over his bed and took down his Qin.

This instrument, a little over three and a half feet (one meter) long, was lined with seven strings with movable bridges. The seven strings represented yin and yang as well as the five elements. It was an ancient classical instrument which Chinese scholars and hermits had been using for several thousand years already, though it was thought to date back twice that long, created by the ancient shaman king, Fuxi. The top of the Qin was round, symbolizing heaven. The bottom was angular and stood for the earth. In this way the shape of the instrument represented the Chinese idea of the cosmos.

He placed it on the small table in front of him and then, raising his hand and breathing deeply, "from the bottom of his feet," he began to play.

17

A Few Last Words

When most people drink tea, they are not aware that some meaningful universal secret is hidden within the drinking pattern. Drinking is not merely drinking. As our hearts connect with the tea during the drinking, it becomes a much different experience. This is the spirit of tea.[1]

Meditation is the gift you can give to yourself of quiet, uninterrupted time, you relax your body, and calm your mind and by doing so gain better control over your thoughts and your life. For millions of people for centuries, mindful preparation of tea and drinking it with intent has been a form of meditation that brings positive results for mind, body and spirit.[2]

Now it is time to rinse our teapot and cup, put our tea back up on the shelf and enter our day anew. I hope this small book has inspired you to learn a bit more about the Way of Tea and how it impacts every aspect of our life.

We have explored the world of *wu wei*—of being natural and flexible—and how what might seem to the world to be worthless can actually be priceless. We have experienced how slowing down can allow us to savor each moment of our life and we have seen how the world of Zen Mind is the same as Tea Mind.

We have traveled with a few of the ancient tea masters from China and Japan and seen how the practice of the Way of Tea brought them to a sense of connection and communion with the Dao or Buddha Mind. Remember, Tea Mind *is* Buddha Mind. The Way of Tea is the way of the Dao, which, though empty in nature, sustains the ten thousand beings.

I hope that you will take the time to enjoy your tea and that you will be able to apply these ancient principles to your life. Remember, the Way of Tea encompasses much more than simply drinking tea. In our world of constant rushing activity it is good to be able to take some time out of the race and bask in the glory of just "being."

Laozi says:

> Who can be still while the muddy water settles?
> Who can remain still until the time comes for action?
>
> (Chapter 15)

By maintaining our still center, even in the midst of activity, we will be better able to flow with the changes that happen in our lives. By using the watercourse way to adapt to whatever container or experience we find ourselves in we can often rise above our stresses and fears.

Lastly I would like to leave you with a few words from the ancient Daoist sage, Zhuangzi, as translated by Gia-Fu Feng and Jane English:

> Do not seek fame. Do not make plans. Do not
> be absorbed by activities. Do not think that you
> know. Be aware of all that is and dwell in the

infinite. Wander where there is no path. Be all that heaven gave you, but act as though you have received nothing. Be empty, that is all.[3]

Notes

1. Zhongxian Wu (2009) *Seeing the Spirit of The Book of Change*, p.46.
2. Theresa Cheung (2007) *Tea Bliss*, p.156.
3. Gia-Fu Feng and Jane English (1974) *Chuang Tsu: The Inner Chapters*, p.159.

Sources for Tea

The Tao of Tea

Address: 3430 S.E. Belmont Street, Portland, OR 97214, USA. Telephone: 503 736 0198. Website: www.taooftea.com (accessed 7 October 2009). This is my favorite teahouse (actually one of two, the other is in the beautiful Classical Chinese Garden in downtown Portland). They carry tea from all over the world and have a very funky, comfortable and charming atmosphere.

Ten Ren Tea

Address: 419 Eccles Avenue, South San Francisco, CA 94080, USA. Telephone: 888 650 1047. Website: www.tenrentea.com (accessed 7 October 2009). This is an old tea company in San Francisco. I like them because they, like teashops in China, sell different grades of each tea. (I usually get the next to the most expensive and am happy with that.)

J-Tea International

Address: 2778 Friendly St, Eugene, OR 97405, USA. Telephone: 541 285 8997. Website: www.jteainternational.com (accessed 7 October 2009). One of my neighbors. Josh Chamberlain is especially knowledgeable about teas from Taiwan.

Sacred Teachings

"Enjoy the teachings on timelessness." Website: www.sacredtea-chings.com (accessed 7 October 2009).

Oolongtea.org

Website started by noted author Daniel Reid, which carries organic High Mountain Oolong Tea and has lots of information on the Way of Tea.

Other sources

Australia
www.oolong-tea.org (accessed 4 January 2010).

Taiwan
www.potterytea.com (accessed 4 January 2010).

United Kingdom
www.allabouttea.co.uk (accessed 4 January 2010).
www.cantonteaco.com (accessed 4 January 2010).

My own site
www.abodetao.com (accessed 4 January 2010).

Bibliography

Blackman, S. (2005) *Graceful Exits: How Great Beings Die.——Death Stories of Hindu, Tibetan Buddhist and Zen Masters.* Boston, MA: Shambhala.

Blofeld, J. (1985) *The Chinese Art of Tea.* London: Allen & Unwin.

Cheung, T. (2007) *Tea Bliss: Infuse Your Life with Health, Wisdom and Contentment.* Berkeley, CA: Conari. 1-800-423-7087, Red Wheel Weiser.

Chow, K. and Kramer, I. (1990) *All the Tea in China.* San Francisco, CA: China Books and Periodicals.

Cohen, K.S. (1997) *The Way of Qigong: The Art and Science of Chinese Energy Healing.* New York, NY: Ballantine.

Feng, G.-F. and English, J. (1974) *Chuang Tsu: The Inner Chapters.* New York, NY: Knopf/Vintage.

Giles, H.A. (1926) *Chuang-Tzu: Mystic, Moralist, and Social Reformer.* Shanghai: Kelly&Walsh.

Girardot, N.J. (1983) *Myth and Meaning in Early Daoism.* Berkeley, CA: University of California Press.

Graham, A.C. (1960) *The Book of Lieh Tzu.* New York, NY: Columbia University Press.

Heiss, M.L. and Heiss, R.J. (2007) *The Story of Tea.* Berkeley, CA: Ten Speed Press.

Hirota, D. (1995) *Wind in the Pines.* Fremont, CA: Asian Humanities Press.

Hohenegger, B. (2006) *Liquid Jade: The Story of Tea from East to West.* New York, NY: St. Martin's Press.

Juniper, A. (2003) *Wabi Sabi: The Japanese Art of Impermanence.* Boston, MA: Tuttle Publishing.

Kaltnemark, M. (1969) *Laozi and Daoism.* Stanford, CA: Stanford University Press.

Lu Yu (1974) *The Classic of Tea*, translated and introduced by F.R. Carpenter. New Jersey: Ecco Press.

Macfarlane, A. and Macfarlane, I. (2004) *Green Gold: The Empire of Tea*. London: Ebury Press.

Merton, T. (1965) *The Way of Chuang Tzu*. New York, NY: New Directions.

Mitscher, L.A. and Dolby, V. (1998) *The Green Tea Book: China's Fountain of Youth*. Garden City, NY: Avery.

Mortenson, G. and Relin, D.O. (2006) *Three Cups of Tea: One Man's Misssion to Fight Terrorism and Build Nations...One School at a Time*. New York, NY: Viking.

Murphy, F.H. (2008) *The Spirit of Tea*. Santa Fe, NM: Sherman Asher.

Ni, H.-C. (1979a) *Tao: The Subtle Universal Law and the Integral Way of Life*. Los Angeles, CA: Shrine of the Eternal Breath of Tao.

Ni, H.-C. (1979b) *The Taoist Inner View of the Universe and the Immortal Realm*. Available from www.taostar.com

Ni, H.-C. (1987) *The Gentle Path of Spiritual Progress*. Los Angeles, CA: Shrine of the Eternal Breath of Tao.

Okakura, K. (2001) *The Book of Tea*. Boston, MA: Shambhala.

Reps, P. and Senzaki, N. (1957) *Zen Flesh, Zen Bones*. Boston, MA: Tuttle Publishing.

Spence, J.D. (2007) *Return to Dragon Mountain*. New York, NY: Viking.

Suzuki, S. (1970) *Zen Mind, Beginner's Mind*. New York, NY: John Weatherhill.

Tanaka, S. (1973) *The Tea Ceremony*. Tokyo, New York and San Francisco: Kodansha International.

Towler, S. (2005) *Tales from the Tao*. London: Watkins.

Waltham, C. (1971) *Chuang Tzu: Genius of the Absurd*. New York, NY: Ace.

Wang Yi'e (2006) *Daoism in China*. Warren, CT: Floating World.

Watts, A. (1975) *Tao: The Watercourse Way*. New York, NY: Pantheon.

Yates, J. (2005) *Tales of a Tea Leaf*. New York, NY: Square One.

Yu-Lan, F. (1973) *A History of Chinese Philosophy: Volume 1*. Princeton, NY: Princeton University Press.

Zhongxian Wu (2009) *Seeking the Spirit of The Book of Change* London: Singing Dragon.

Zhongxian Wu (2008) *Vital Breath of the Dao*. London: Singing Dragon.

About the Author

Solala Towler was born in 1950 in Massachusetts and currently lives in Eugene, Oregon. He is editor, since 1993, of *The Empty Vessel: The Journal of Daoist Philosophy and Practice*. He is author of *A Gathering of Cranes: Bringing the Dao to the West* (The Abode of the Eternal Dao, 1996); *Embarking On the Way: A Guide to Western Daoism* (The Abode of the Eternal Dao, 1997); *Dao Paths to Love, Dao Paths to Good Fortune, Dao Paths to Harmony* and *Dao Paths to Long Life* (MQP Publications (London) and Andrews McMeel (USA), 2002); *Chi: Energy of Harmony* and *Chi: Energy of Happiness* (MQP Publications (London), and Andrews McMeel (USA), 2002); and *Tales of the Dao* (Watkins (London), 2005). His work has also been translated into Dutch, French and Spanish.

Solala is an instructor of Daoist meditation and of several styles of qigong, including Soaring Crane Qigong, Essence Qigong and Wuji Qigong. He has taught classes and seminars all over the United States and elsewhere and is past president of the National Qigong Association USA. He leads tours to China and Tibet to study qigong, and to visit Daoist temples in the sacred mountains of China as well as monasteries in Tibet.

Solala is the founding member of the sacred music ensemble Windhorse and has recorded four CDs of music for yoga, tai chi, qigong and meditation, *Mountain Gate, Sacred Soundings, Windhorse: Spirit of Tibet* and *Boundless.* His music has been used as a soundtrack in eight videos and DVDs about tai chi and qigong.

To find out more about Solala's work visit his website at www. abodetao.com or write to him at solala@abodetao.com.